Android for Work

Productivity for Professionals

Marziah Karch

Apress®

Android for Work: Productivity for Professionals

ISBN-13 (pbk): 978-1-4302-3000-7

ISBN-13 (electronic): 978-1-4302-3001-4

Printed and bound in the United States of America 9 8 7 6 5 4 3 2 1

President and Publisher: Paul Manning
Lead Editor: Steve Anglin
Development Editor: Douglas Pundick
Technical Reviewer: Massimo Nardone
Editorial Board: Clay Andres, Steve Anglin, Mark Beckner, Ewan Buckingham, Gary Cornell, Jonathan Gennick, Jonathan Hassell, Michelle Lowman, Matthew Moodie, Duncan Parkes, Jeffrey Pepper, Frank Pohlmann, Douglas Pundick, Ben Renow-Clarke, Dominic Shakeshaft, Matt Wade, Tom Welsh
Coordinating Editor: Mary Tobin
Copy Editor: Damon Larson
Compositor: MacPS, LLC
Indexer: Potomac Indexing, LLC
Artist: April Milne
Cover Designer: Anna Ishchenko

Distributed to the book trade worldwide by Springer Science+Business Media, LLC., 233 Spring Street, 6th Floor, New York, NY 10013. Phone 1-800-SPRINGER, fax (201) 348-4505, e-mail orders-ny@springer-sbm.com, or visit www.springeronline.com.

For information on translations, please e-mail rights@apress.com, or visit www.apress.com.

Apress and friends of ED books may be purchased in bulk for academic, corporate, or promotional use. eBook versions and licenses are also available for most titles. For more information, reference our Special Bulk Sales–eBook Licensing web page at www.apress.com/info/bulksales.

Contents at a Glance

Contents

About the Author

Marziah Karch enjoys the challenge of explaining complex technology to beginning audiences. She is an education technologist for Johnson County Community College in the Kansas City metro area with over ten years of experience. She holds a master's degree in instructional design and has taught credit courses in interactive media. Marziah also contributes to the *New York Times*-owned About.com and has been its "Guide to Google" since 2006. When she's not feeding her geek side with new gadgets or writing about technology, Marziah enjoys life in Lawrence, Kansas, with her husband Harold and her two children.

About the Technical Reviewer

Massimo Nardone was born under the Vesuvius, and he holds a master of science degree in computing science from the University of Salerno, Italy. He currently works as a Senior IT Security and Infrastructure Architect and Finnish Invention Development Team Leader for IBM Finland, and is an Open Group Master Certified IT Architect. He works as the IT lead architect and handles security responsibilities including IT infrastructure, security auditing and assessment, PKI/WPKI, secure tunneling, LDAP security, and SmartCard security.

With more than 16 years of work experience in mobile, security, and web technology for both national and international projects, Massimo has worked as a project manager, software engineer, research engineer, chief security architect, and software specialist. He has been a visiting lecturer and supervisor for the Security of Communication Protocols course at the Networking Laboratory of the Helsinki University of Technology (TKK). He is very familiar with security communication protocol testing tools and methodologies, he has developed Internet and mobile applications for many different technologies, and he has used many programming languages.

He also works as a security application auditing expert, checking on new application vulnerabilities, utilizing security standards such as ISO 17799 and ISO 27001 (formal BS 7799:2).

Massimo has worked as a technical reviewer for many different IT book publishers in areas such as IT security, web technology, and databases. He has researched, designed, and implemented security methodologies in areas including Standard BS7799, PKI and WPKI, Java (JAAS, JSSE, JCE, etc.), BEA WebLogic, J2EE, LDAP, SSO, Apache, SQL Server, XML, and SmartCard.

He currently holds four international patents, in the PKI, SIP, SAML, and proxy fields.

Acknowledgments

This book wouldn't have been possible without my supportive husband, Harold. Thank you for minding the kids and rebuilding the basement while I holed myself up in the bedroom and wrote all the time. It's good to see you again.

Thank you to Steve Anglin, Mary Tobin, Douglas Pundick, and everyone at Apress for guiding me through this whole book-writing process. You all rock.

I'd also like to thank Jonathan Bacon, Barry Bailey, Paul Decelles, and Melissa Wisler for letting me play with their personal phones. Melissa gets an extra thanks for shooting my author photo.

Customer service at the Lawrence Kansas Sprint, T-Mobile, Best Buy, and Verizon stores all deserve praise for answering questions and letting me play with the phones—even when they knew I wasn't there to buy. Thanks also go to all the vendors and representatives at CES who answered my questions and allowed me to take photos of their products.

Other people who helped along the way include Chris McKitterick and Sarah Scalet for helping me decide if this was a feasible project, and Sean Carlson at Google for inadvertently putting the book-writing bug in my brain.

Thank you also goes to HTC for permission to use their photos.

Portions of this book are reproductions or modifications of work created and shared by Google and used according to terms described in the Creative Commons 3.0 Attribution License.

Preface

This book was written mainly for the mobile office worker who wants to check work e-mail and maybe tether Wi-Fi with a laptop while still getting the most out of the fun features in Android. You don't need to be a programmer or computer whiz to use this book, and there should hopefully be enough goodies here for both the new and veteran Android owner.

Android is still innovating very rapidly, both from operating system (OS) upgrades and phone vendor modifications, and new Android-based phones are being released all the time. This book was written mainly using a Google Nexus One running Android 2.1 and 2.2. The Nexus One model was both powerful and carrier neutral, so it seemed an ideal choice.

I've tried to make note of any variations between phones, OS versions, and carriers, but there are going to be times where what I describe is not quite the same as what you see on your screen. In most cases, these should be minor differences.

It's been very exciting to see Android grow as I wrote this, and it will be even more exciting to see how it does in the future. I hope this book serves as a useful reference to getting the most out of your Android phone.

Chapter 1

Buying and Activating an Android Phone

ChangeWave is a research network that examines technological trends for investors through surveys and focus groups. According to a ChangeWave survey, 6 percent of those surveyed wanted their next phone to run Android in September of 2009. Three months later, 21 percent of users wanted one. Only 4 percent of those surveyed actually *had* an Android phone. That's quite a leap for an operating system (OS) that was only available on one phone the year prior.

Android is a relative newcomer to the phone market, yet this mobile OS is already being introduced on phones by virtually every phone manufacturer and major US wireless company. It's flexible, fun, and boasts thousands of apps. It doesn't hurt that Google released the OS for free.

In this chapter, you'll learn what to look for when purchasing an Android phone and how to activate and start using your phone. You'll also learn how to read Microsoft Exchange e-mail on your phone, and how to pick a phone with minimal security standards for business use.

The History of Android

Back in 2005, Google bought a small startup company founded by Andy Ruben, the founder of Danger, Inc. Danger is best known for creating the T-Mobile-branded Sidekick phones. Rubin's new company, Android, also included Richard Minor from Orange (a UK phone company), Chris White from WebTV, and Andy McFadden from WebTV and Moxi. Android was a bit of a mystery. It made software for mobile, but Google didn't provide any details or plans for Android going forward.

After rumors that Google would be releasing its own iPhone competitor, Google instead introduced a new phone OS. On November 5, 2007, Google announced the Android OS and the Open Handset Alliance, a group of companies that would help develop it. Open

Handset Alliance members include phone carriers, software developers, device manufacturers, and component makers.

Android had a very different philosophy when compared to Apple and the iPhone. Anyone could use Android in their devices for free, anyone could modify Android, and anyone could develop apps for it without seeking permission to put their apps in the Android Market. Google also seeded the Android app market by holding developer contests with cash prizes, so by the time the first Android phone arrived in stores, there was a selection of apps available for download. Figure 1–1 shows the T-Mobile G1, the first Android phone to hit the market.

Figure 1–1. *T-Mobile G1*

Today Android is moving beyond the phone. It's powering eBook readers, tablets, and even medical devices. The cost and easy customization lend it to all sorts of applications for portable devices.

Is it good for business users? Absolutely. Just as the iPhone gained popularity with consumers before it became a legitimate business choice, Android phones are becoming consumer favorites with serious business apps following closely behind. Because Android allows a high level of customization, large enterprise deployments can even create a phone uniquely suited to the needs of their employees.

Selecting the Right Phone

Mobile phones used to be devices that made calls. Today they're small computers capable of sending and receiving e-mail, browsing the Internet, and running software. Unlike the desktop computer market, Windows does not have the most market share in the mobile phone market. Internationally, Nokia dominates the market with the now open source Symbian platform, but in the United States, Symbian just hasn't caught on.

InformationWeek surveyed 695 businesses in November 2009. BlackBerry was the most popular platform, followed by iPhone and Windows Mobile. Survey respondents reported Android use in enterprises at 6 percent. The report is available at http://mobile-applications.informationweek.com/.

That 6 percent may seem small, but technology research firm Gartner expects Android to be the second most popular phone platform in the world by 2012. If you're looking at Android, consider yourself a trendsetter.

Once you've decided to go with an Android phone, you need to decide *which* Android phone is right for you. There are a lot of choices, and it's not as simple as picking from a set of hardware features. Android devices come in all shapes and sizes, and some companies offer custom user interfaces, apps, or other enhancements.

Android Phone Variations

Using a default Android installation makes it easier to receive upgrades to the OS, but sometimes it also means you miss out on some fantastic features. This isn't a comprehensive list, but here are a few of the phone offerings on the market along with the Android variations they contain.

An important feature for business users is the ability to natively sync with Exchange accounts—that is, the ability to use the *ActiveSync protocol*. Another important feature is the ability to erase sensitive data from the phone if it is lost or stolen. This is called a *remote wipe*. You won't find either of them as standard Android features as of Android 2.1, but they are included in Android 2.2. You can purchase apps for those features, but it's not as nice as something that just works out of the box.

> **TIP:** If the phone says "With Google" on the back, that indicates it is running a pure Android OS. The phone carrier may have added some bonus software, but there won't be any modifications to the phone OS itself.

HTC and Sense

HTC makes a variety of Android phones, including the first Android phone on the market, the T-Mobile G1/HTC Dream. It also makes the Google Nexus One. Some phones use a vanilla Android installation, and some include HTC's enhancement, *Sense*.

Sense is a user interface system based around widgets. Widgets are small, always-on applications that run on your phone Home screen for specific purposes, like showing weather information or posting Twitter updates. This is similar to Windows Gadgets on desktop computers. When Android 1.6 was only offering three screens for customization, Sense offered seven. The screens use "scenes" centered around common activities, such as work and social media, and HTC created several custom widgets to make using phone activities easier. Sense also ties some information together, such as combining phone contact information and Facebook.

Sense phones do sync with Exchange e-mail accounts, and the e-mail widget makes checking business e-mail easy. Sense phones come with a PDF reader, which is very handy for reading attachments. It's also easier to use Sense phones for web browsing, because Sense allows for common two-finger gestures like pinching to shrink pages. Multitouch gestures are supported by Android, but Google elected to turn off this feature until Android 2.1.

Enterprise security sometimes demands the ability to remove all the Exchange or other sensitive data from your phone if the phone is lost or stolen (as mentioned previously, this is known as a remote wipe). Sense does not support remote wipe natively prior to Android 2.2, so you'll have to use a third-party app if you need this level of protection for your business data.

HTC Sense phones include the Hero and Tattoo phones. HTC Android phones without Sense include the G1/HTC Dream, the myTouch/Magic, and the Google Nexus One. Although they don't come with Sense, these phones do come with exclusive software from the phone carrier.

That said, the G1 and myTouch are the oldest Android phone offerings. Hardware has advanced since their release, so don't get locked into a two-year contract with one of those phones unless it's a *very* compelling deal. (For more information, see the unofficial wiki at `http://androidonhtc.com/`.)

Motorola and MOTOBLUR

Motorola may be more responsible for Android's popularity than any other phone manufacturer. The Motorola DROID was heavily advertised as a competitor to the iPhone, and it became the first truly drool-worthy Android phone to hit the market. DROID is also a straightforward Android offering without extra user interface software.

Motorola's user interface enhancement is MOTOBLUR, also known simply as Blur. Blur is meant primarily as a social networking feature that combines feeds from e-mail messages and sites like Twitter, Facebook, and Flickr, and places the messages directly on the Home screen of the phone without requiring you to log into separate apps. MOTOBLUR also allows native syncing with Exchange e-mail accounts and has built-in support for remote wipe. That means if your phone is lost, your private data doesn't have to be vulnerable. (It's worth noting that, when I asked phone manufacturers about remote wipe on Android, Motorola was the only company that offered the feature out of the box.)

Motorola's lineup includes the Moto DROID, which runs a basic Android OS. Their Blur phones include the CLIQ and the BACKFLIP. The BACKFLIP is noteworthy for its unusual design. Rather than a slide-out keyboard, it has a hinged keyboard that flips from the back, as the name implies. The screen is touch sensitive, but so is the area just behind it, so you can scroll through messages without obscuring your view of the screen.

Sony Ericsson and UX

Sony Ericsson entered the Android phone market with the Xperia X10. The X10 has been modified with a user interface called UX (for "user experience"). UX has an intensely graphical interface, including Mediascape and Timescape for browsing through contacts and media files. Timescape and Mediascape aggregate multiple streams, such as Twitter posts, e-mails, picture posts, and status updates. The information is organized chronologically, and when the Infinite button is pressed, all the information for one person or artist is presented for browsing.

The phone has an 8.1-megapixel camera, so it's ideal for anyone who needs to carry a point-and-shoot camera to job sites, such as real estate professionals or contractors. It also has facial recognition software built in to organize those photos.

Sony Ericsson made the interesting choice to include two app markets with their phone. You can either use the standard Android Market or the Sony PlayNow store, for apps geared more specifically toward Xperia X10 phones. The name is slightly confusing, because previous Xperia phones were Windows Mobile based. The X10 and X10 Mini use Android.

The Google Phone

Leading up to Google's introduction of Android, there had been long-standing rumors that Google was going to introduce its own phone, just like Apple did with the iPhone. In January 2010, they did exactly that, and made the curious choice to compete against other phone manufacturers in the Android OS phone market they'd created. Figure 1–2 shows the Nexus One, the first official Google phone. Although it's made by HTC, the phone is branded and sold by Google.

Figure 1–2. *The Nexus One*

Is there anything special about the Nexus One? Yes and no. It's a nice phone, and it runs Android 2.1 on hardware designed specifically for that purpose. It includes voice-to-text dictation, and it includes a nice GPS navigator for turn-by-turn directions. As an official Google product, it will likely be first in line for Android OS upgrades.

That said, there are plenty of other Android offerings worth serious consideration. The Nexus One is no longer being sold by Google. The Nexus One was not a big hit with consumers, who prefer to play with phones before they purchase them, and Google shuttered the online Nexus One store in July of 2010.

Touchscreen vs. Keyboard

One way you can narrow your choices is by deciding if you're a keyboard or a touchscreen person. Personally, I'm a touchscreen person, but I've known many people that can't stand to enter text without a physical keyboard on their phone.

- *Keyboard*: If you feel uncomfortable with virtual keyboards, such as those on the iPhone, you should go with a keyboard model. Keyboards can slide out, such as those on the T-Mobile G1 and the Verizon DROID, or they can flip out like the one on the Motorola BACKFLIP.

- Keyboards add bulk to a phone, but they're nice to have around when you need them. Even if you have a keyboard, you can still use the virtual keyboard if you choose.

- *No Keyboard*: Ditching the keyboard keeps the phone slimmer and often means you'll get a better-quality screen. It also means you have less to go wrong with your phone physically. The Google Nexus One, Xperia X10, and HTC EVO all skip the slide-out keyboard. The HTC EVO even allows you to do part of your text entry with your voice.

NOTE: Before you settle on a phone model, make sure you try typing a significant chunk of text in the store. Does the keyboard respond well? Are the keys easy to reach? Do they light up in the dark? Likewise, you want to make sure virtual keyboards are responsive and large enough to accommodate your fingers.

Phone Optics

Do you need to take on-site pictures or video as part of your work duties? If so, you'll need to make sure you select a phone with a good camera. The Xperia X10, HTC EVO and DROID Incredible take the largest photos at the time of this publication, but other phones such as the HTC Hero, DROID, and Nexus One have 5-megapixel cameras with flash, which would be adequate for many camera tasks.

You can also download software like Camera Pro to extend your photo-taking abilities.

Avoid phones with smaller cameras or no flash, like the G1, myTouch, and Tattoo.

Android Devices That Aren't Phones

One of the more interesting uses for Android has been in devices that aren't even phones. Android powers eBook readers and netbooks (and it could even power your microwave). If you have regular access to Wi-Fi and don't mind taking an extra device with you, you may not need to buy a full smartphone in order to take advantage of Android.

Here's a few of those non-phones powered by Android.

The Alex is a simple eBook reader with an E-ink screen on top and an Android touchscreen on the bottom. E-ink is the patented display technology behind the Amazon Kindle and many other eBook readers. It's a form of electronic paper that looks great in full sunlight and requires low power usage. This device uses Wi-Fi to download books, but it can also run built-in Android apps. This would be a good choice for people familiar with Android on their phone or people who want to give Android a whirl without committing to a phone plan. The Barnes & Noble Nook also runs on Android, but it is heavily modified.

Android Readers

The enTourage eDGe is a device that opens like a book. On one side is an E-ink screen that can be used with a stylus for note taking, and on the other side is a keyboardless netbook that runs on Android. The device is marketed toward education students as a textbook replacement, but there's mainstream appeal to the device as well.

It runs Android apps and includes DataVis Documents To Go software, which allows it to open Microsoft Office documents. Although it ships without a keyboard, you could use a USB keyboard to do heavy typing.

enTourage is planning on a 3G release at a future date, so the device itself with a USB microphone and a VoIP (Voice over IP) app may take the place of a phone, depending on the price of data plans.

For more information on the enTourage eDGe, visit www.entourageedge.com/.

Multimedia Players

The M7 is a multimedia player from Cydle. Think of it as a netbook without a keyboard, or a large-screen smartphone without the phone. It's a bit large to carry in your pocket, but at $199 it's priced very well to be a home or office digital photo frame that reminds you of appointments or allows you to check e-mail.

Netbooks

Cydle is also one of many companies offering Android-powered netbooks. From extremely tiny to extremely cheap, the 2010 Consumer Electronics Show was full of companies hoping to sell netbooks and trying to use the free OS to give themselves a competitive edge for pricing.

CAUTION: I'd warn you against using Android as a netbook OS for any device that doesn't have a touchscreen. Android was never meant to run on systems without touchscreens, and such devices don't work as well as a netbook running Ubuntu Linux or Microsoft Windows. Google is rolling out Chrome OS for netbooks and other larger computers.

Microwaves, Washing Machines, and Printers (Oh My!)

Touch Revolution makes an Android-powered touch interface for other companies called the NIM1000. Touch Revolution is an *original design manufacturer (ODM)*, which means they create products for other companies to brand as their own. You'll never see Touch Revolution on the interface, but a representative told me that their technology was being used to create Android-powered interfaces for medical devices and the back of airline seats.

Touch Revolution picked Android because it's easily customizable and free. Touch Revolution also felt Android was better designed than Windows CE. Figure 1–3 shows the Touch Revolution interface. To prove the versatility of its design, Touch Revolution demonstrated an Android-powered washing machine, microwave, printer, and enterprise phone set. That doesn't mean anyone will *actually* use Android to determine the length of their spin cycle. However, people are likely to use Android interfaces on devices that have nothing in common with phones.

Figure 1–3. *A prototype microwave interface powered by Android*

Understanding Phone Plans

In order to use an Android phone, you must have a data plan, and there's no point in getting a metered plan if you can avoid it, although recently phone companies have moved away from unlimited plans. You'll use the network every time you use the phone for anything other than talking. Go for unlimited access if you can. Some companies charge more for smartphone data plans than they do for data access on regular phones, so be sure to ask before you commit.

You do not need an SMS (Short Message Service) texting service to use an Android phone, but many plans bundle the service with the data plan. If you plan on using your phone as a portable Wi-Fi hotspot, you may also need to purchase a plan that includes it.

Android phones generally have two prices. One price is the actual cost of the phone, and the other price is the price when purchased with a contract. The reason phones are cheaper with a contract is because the phone carrier charges you more each month to make up for the price of the phone.

Often you end up paying less overall when you buy a phone with contract, but it does mean you're locked into that contract and may not be able to switch services, upgrade phones, or cut back on minutes without facing a penalty. Consult with an accountant on the tax implications of a subsidized plan over buying a phone outright.

Generally, the price of Android phones without subsidy is around $400 to $600. The price with a contract is around $100 to $200. Buying an Android phone at cost will generally save you around $20 a month on your phone bill.

> **TIP:** Ask your phone carrier if it offers a workplace discount. Many companies have agreements with phone carriers that will get you a better deal.

Activating Your Phone

You do not need an activation key to activate an Android phone, but you do need a Google account.

Different Android phones have different activation sequences, but all of them involve logging in with your Google account. If you don't have one already, create a Google account with a Gmail address by registering at `http://mail.google.com/mail/signup`.

If your workplace uses Google Apps for Enterprise, you could use this ID as your Google account, but, unless this phone is part of an enterprise deployment, the wiser course of action is to use a personal Google account and add the Google Apps information as an additional e-mail account. That way you don't lose your phone data if you switch jobs.

Transferring Your Contacts

If you're upgrading phones, you need to get your contact information from one phone to the other. If you can get the data to Google Contacts at `www.google.com/contacts`, it will appear on your phone. Export your contacts as a CVS or vCard file, and then use the import link on the upper-right corner of the Google Contacts page. This will work for Outlook and the Apple Address Book.

You may also be able to import contacts from your SIM card using the menu option in your contacts list. I'll talk more about the contacts list in Chapter 4.

If you can't export contacts from your phone, you can still enter them on your computer more easily than you can your phone.

Using Google Accounts

I'll talk about this in greater detail in Chapters 2 and 3, but virtually everything on Android phones is handled through your Google account. You should set up and explore these tools on the Web for a better understanding of how they work on your phone.

If you purchase apps in the Android Market, you'll use your Google account and Google Checkout to complete the transaction. The default e-mail account is Gmail, and the default calendar is Google Calendar.

Here are a few of the default Google services you'll get to know as you use your phone:

- *Gmail*: Gmail is a free web-based e-mail service, but it's good enough to replace those e-mail accounts your Internet service provider gives you. I'll talk about e-mail in greater detail in Chapter 6. Make sure you register for an account. Some Android phones will not let you activate them without it.

- *Google Calendar*: Google Calendar works a bit differently from Outlook's calendar. It has standard features like events and invitations, but it is meant to be even more collaborative. You manage Google Calendar by adding multiple "calendars" and sharing them with others. For instance, you can have a calendar you allow colleagues to see but not edit, a calendar team members can all edit, and another calendar of fully public events.

- *Google Maps*: You're probably already familiar with this map application. Google Maps is the engine behind most of your phone's geographically sensitive apps. Not only can Google Maps give you driving directions, but it can also give you walking and public transport directions. This is invaluable when you're on the road.

- *Google Checkout*: Google Checkout is a tool for buyers and merchants to complete credit card transactions without revealing the credit card info to the merchant. It's a competitor to PayPal. You'll need to set up an account with credit card information if you want to purchase apps from the Android Market.

- *Picasa*: Picasa Web Albums is Google's answer to Flickr. If you want to upload pictures from your phone to the Web, this is the default location for sharing. You may want to set up your account with albums and public or private sharing permissions if you need to share photos as part of your job. It's more efficient to upload photos to Picasa than it is to send them as e-mail attachments, though you can do both. Picasa also has a desktop program you can use for syncing and editing photos.

- *YouTube*: If you have any reason to take quick videos with your phone, set up a YouTube account with your preferred username beforehand. You can upload videos directly instead of offloading them to your desktop computer first.

Setting Up Exchange

If your workplace uses Google Apps for Enterprise, configuration is easy. However, most workplaces still run on Microsoft Exchange.

You'll have two e-mail apps on your phone. One is for Gmail, and the other is simply called "Email." On most Android phones, it's represented by a simple yellow envelope with an @ sticking out of it. This is the app you need to use for non-Gmail accounts.

If your phone supports Microsoft ActiveSync, setup is straightforward: use the Exchange settings your IT department supplies you and set up your account. Android 2.2 includes Exchange support, and many phone manufacturers have included Exchange support in earlier, modified versions of Android, such as MOTOBLUR on some Motorola phones and Sense UI on some HTC phones.

Phones with pure Android do not officially support ActiveSync in versions prior to Android 2.2. However, that doesn't mean you can't use them to check your Exchange e-mail through third-party apps.

POP Access

If your system administrator allows it, you can use POP or IMAP access with your Exchange account. Just use the settings your administrator supplies. However, you're not going to get calendar and task syncing this way.

To add calendar sync, you can download the free Google Calendar Sync tool: http://dl.google.com/googlecalendarsync/GoogleCalendarSync_Installer.exe.

Install Google Calendar Sync on a desktop computer you use for Outlook. Choose your syncing option. You can choose a two-way sync to share dates in both directions, or you can choose one-way syncing from Outlook or Google.

Your workplace may not allow you to install software on your desktop computer, so be sure to ask beforehand.

Outlook Web Access

You can use Outlook Web Access (OWA) with the web browser that comes with your phone. This is probably not the most desirable way to check your e-mail, but it will work in a pinch. If your business has stringent legal concerns about data security (such as the medical industry), your IT department may require most or all phones to use OWA access only. It's not out of laziness or spite, even if it makes checking your e-mail more difficult. You can make life a little easier by creating a shortcut to your OWA login page. This is covered in a later Chapter 10.

Access Using Third-Party Apps

If the first two options will not work for you, you can turn to third-party apps for the solution. Exchange by TouchDown is a $20 app from NitroDesk that allows Exchange ActiveSync with push e-mail. NitroDesk also offers a free trial—take advantage of this to make sure it works with your Exchange service. It is not supported with some Exchange Server 2003 configurations.

If you use TouchDown, you'll have a separate e-mail, calendar, and task list. It's all familiar for Outlook users, but it doesn't sync this data with your Google Calendar. You can download TouchDown from the Android Market or by visiting www.nitrodesk.com/.

There's also the free HTC WorkEmail app available at www.nexeo.net/android/Mail.apk. Unlike TouchDown, it does not support Exchange calendar syncing, so this will only work for retrieving your e-mail.

Summary

Android is a flexible and fun phone platform that is also very useful for work, though some phones and configurations may not support your specific workplace security protocols. The flexibility of Android and the variety of phones available make selecting the right phone more complicated than picking a color and carrier.

In order to use Android, you must have a Google account, and some Android phones require a Gmail account as well. Register and create a Gmail account before you activate your phone.

Syncing with Exchange is easier on some Android phones than it is on others, but thanks to third-party apps, it should be possible to use Exchange with any Android phone. Android allows open access to the Android Market for developers, and it allows Android phones to install Android-compatible apps from other app stores or individuals.

Chapter 2

Using Your Phone for the First Time

As discussed in Chapter 1, Android phones do not come in a few simple varieties. Phone manufacturers are free to make a wide variety of modifications to the size, shape, and software options available on each phone. Some Android devices aren't even phones.

You'll want to get to know your hardware when you use your phone, so in this chapter I'll go over some of the buttons most Android phones use and the basic interface. I'll also touch briefly on security and preparing your Android for international use.

SIM Cards

Your SIM card identifies your phone number and identity information for your device. All modern cell phones take them, but they're not created alike. Some phones are *locked* and only accept SIM cards from specific carriers, while others are open devices and will accept any standard SIM. Providers may also be willing to unlock the device after the first year. Be sure to check and see whether you have an open or locked device before you purchase.

Even if you don't plan on switching carriers, an open device has better resale value and allows you more travel options. However, most devices available in the United States are still sold locked to specific carriers, and getting the perfect phone for most situations might have to trump getting a little flexibility on resale.

If you are upgrading your phone with the same carrier, you'll simply transfer your old SIM into your new device. If you're changing phone carriers or buying a cell line for the first time, you'll need to get a new SIM card from your carrier.

Keep in mind that your Google account info is not stored on your SIM card. Your contacts for Android phones are stored on Google's servers. If you're upgrading from a smartphone on a different platform, you can export your contacts and import them into

Google. If you're upgrading from a standard phone, your phone carrier might help you out. You can import your contacts from your SIM card by viewing your contacts in Android and pressing menu: import/export. Otherwise, you should transfer your contacts *before* you switch your SIM card out. Just put them in Google and they'll magically be on your phone.

Some phones may have dual SIM slots to allow for users to separately bill business and personal use or to travel internationally. General Mobile offers an unlocked dual SIM Android phone called the DSTL1.

Physical Buttons

Although different phones have different configurations, most have physical buttons for power and volume control. They also have Home, Menu, Back, and Search buttons, along with a trackball. Some phones also have a Camera button, a green Call button, and a red End Call button. Figure 2–1 is taken from the Android developer's kit, and while you'll never see a phone that looks like this, it shows you the possible physical buttons that could be on your phone.

Figure 2–1. *Buttons*

Home

The Home button, as expected, returns your phone to the Home screen. Android allows multitasking, so you don't have to stop using one app in order to open the next one. This is important to note because *pressing the Home button isn't the same as pressing a quit button*. Your app could still be running and still draining your battery in the background.

However, if you want to check the weather or send an e-mail and then get right back to that important web page you were reading, using the Home button is a great way to get there.

Back

The Back button is a multipurpose button. The default action for the Back button is that it will quit whatever is on the screen. Usually that means it will go back to the previous screen, go back to the previous web site, or quit the app and go back to the Home screen.

That's the default action, but programmers are free to override it. That means sometimes you might think you've quit an app when really you've just gone to the Home screen while leaving the app on in the background. This isn't always a bad thing. You want alarm clocks and e-mail programs to still work in the background.

However, there are some apps you'll need to explicitly close through the menu rather than just using the Back button. If you notice memory problems or abnormal battery use, check to make sure you don't have resource-hogging apps running after you thought you'd quit them.

Search

The Search button does just what you'd think it would do. It opens up a search box. The Search button doesn't just search the Web. It also searches items on your phone. This is very handy if you're looking for an e-mail message that could be in one of three inboxes, or trying to find an elusive app you've downloaded.

Menu

The Menu button is the Android equivalent of right-clicking. It gives you a context-sensitive menu of options that apply to whatever is running on your screen. The Menu button options vary by application, so some Menu options are more helpful than others. If you're ever stuck trying to find an option, try pressing the Menu button.

Scroll/Select

All Android phones to date have a physical trackball as well as a touchscreen. This is good news for anyone who feels a little fat-fingered at times. The appearance of the trackball varies, but it's generally pretty simple. Move left, right, up, and down as the screen highlights your choices. Press down in the center of the trackball to make a selection.

Volume

On most phones, the volume controls are on the side. If you notice your phone is freezing while you're trying to do something like take a photo, double-check that you're not holding down the volume button.

Camera

Some phones have a physical Camera button that launches the Android Camera app, but you can also just launch the camera from the app menu. Newer phones no longer bother with the button.

Once your camera is launched, you'll see a basic camera interface. Figure 2–2 shows the camera controls in Android 2.1. On most phones, tilting the phone rotates the camera for either landscape or portrait mode. The top-left square shows the last photo or video you shot, the toggle at the middle right allows you to switch between video and camera modes, and the button at the bottom right starts shooting pictures or video.

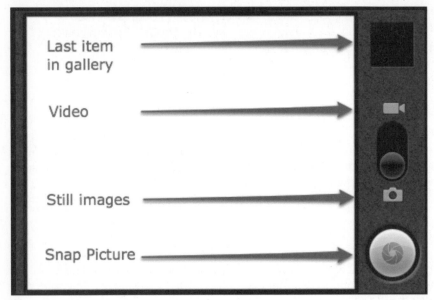

Figure 2–2. *Camera*

Android cameras generally have autofocus, but don't expect this to be *perfect* focus. This isn't a substitute for a single-lens reflex (SLR) camera. That said, you can get surprisingly good pictures from Android phones. You just have to keep a few things in mind. Most cameras come with a delay you'd think was way too long in a dedicated point-and-shoot. Use this to your advantage. Pressing the virtual button on your phone makes it shake, so you have a second or so to steady your hand. Anticipate the delay and hold your phone steady.

Navigating the Touchscreen

If you're not used to a touchscreen phone, it may take a bit of practice to navigate. Android phones generally do not come with a stylus, so using your fingernail will not work. I only mention this because I've seen people try it. Use the pad of your finger, just like you'd use on the track pad of your laptop.

Push briefly to select items or launch apps. Selecting a text entry area will open the virtual keyboard.

Drag to move the screen or the item.

You can also mix it up and combine touchscreen navigation with the physical trackball or a physical keyboard. This is handy when you're trying to select something very tiny, like a one-line form on a web site.

Home Screen, Sweet Home Screen

Figure 2–3 shows the default Home screen for Android 2.1. This is where you can store your favorite apps or display your favorite wallpaper. Your phone actually has between three and seven pages of Home screen. With your phone in portrait mode, swipe your finger sideways to flip between the pages of your Home screen.

I'll get more into customization in Chapters 14 and 15. One idea to keep in mind for organization is to keep a theme in mind for every page, so you know where to find the apps you need. One page may be dedicated to social networking apps. One page might be dedicated to e-mail and office productivity while another page might be dedicated to games, restaurants, and entertainment tools.

Figure 2–3. *Home screen*

The App Tray

The app tray holds all of your spare apps. You open the tray by clicking or dragging on the bottom of the screen, depending on which version of Android you're using. In some versions of Android, this looks like a drawer or a tab button, as in Figure 2–3, and you use a dragging motion to pull open the drawer. In others, it looks like a series of small squares clustered together, and you only need to click. Figure 2–4 shows the open app tray on Android 2.1.

Figure 2–4. *The app tray*

Whatever it looks like, it's generally at the bottom of the screen, and this is how you bring up your apps. Once the app tray is open, you can launch apps by clicking them. Click the Back or Home button to return to the Home screen.

The Long Click

If you press down on an item and hold for a few seconds, this is what Android calls a *long click*. You'll generally feel some haptic feedback when you use the long click—the phone will vibrate slightly to let you know that you've done something different than a regular press.

A long click can be programmed into apps, but on the Home screen it is used to add and remove items.

To add an app to your Home screen, do the following:

1. Flick your finger to find the page of the Home screen you want to modify.

2. Open the app tray and find the icon for the app you want to launch.

3. Long-click the app (keep pressing).

4. The app tray will vanish after a few seconds, and you'll see the Home screen.

5. Continue to press down, and drag your app to the desired position.

6. Release your finger.

You can remove apps from Home screens by using a reverse of the same process. Long-click the app from the Home screen until a trash can appears. Drag the app into the trash can. Yes, the trash can. This is the same unfortunate metaphor problem that Macintosh has. Dragging the app into the trash just removes it from the Home screen; it doesn't actually delete the app from your phone.

Switching Between Portrait and Landscape

Your phone screen is a rectangle, and it's reasonable that what you're viewing will affect how you want to view it. On pure Android installations, the Home screens will always be in portrait mode. I asked Google about it, and they told me that this was by design. Once you launch apps, you can shift between portrait and landscape mode.

If you are using a slide-out keyboard, your phone will automatically switch to landscape mode when you open the keyboard. You'd be typing sideways if it didn't, so this is also by design.

If you have a phone with a virtual keyboard, you can switch between portrait and landscape mode by flipping your phone to the desired orientation anywhere but the Home screen. If you have a phone with a keyboard, you'll generally have to force landscape orientation by sliding out the keyboard.

Using the Virtual Keyboard

Your phone may or may not have a physical keyboard, but all Android phones have a virtual keyboard, as shown in Figure 2–5. Selecting any text entry area will open up the virtual keyboard, so long as you don't also have a physical keyboard open when you do it.

Figure 2–5. Keyboard

If you've ever used a virtual keyboard on an iPhone or iPod touch, Android's offering is pretty similar. Press the keys with the meat of your finger to type. When your phone is in landscape mode, you get a wider, more comfortable keyboard.

If you need numbers or symbols, press the ?123 key at the bottom left of the screen. Press the ABC key to return to letters.

On the Nexus One, you'll also see a small microphone button on the keyboard. You can use this for speech-to-text. It's not completely accurate, but it can save you some typing. Speech-to-text requires a data connection, and although the technology is improving, there aren't any options for personalizing voice recognition for an individual speaker beyond your language and locale settings. That means you can differentiate between UK and American English, but you can't differentiate individual American accents.

You may notice that some apps offer slightly different keyboard layouts. You may see @ offered on the main keyboard, or a .com key offered as a choice. This is something that the programmer overrides, so well-designed apps will give you these easy shortcuts.

Zooming In and Out

Zooming views in and out depends on the phone you use. Some phones have multitouch support built into the browser, and some do not. Android 2.2 on the Nexus One allows the two-finger pinch to zoom motions that iPhone users have always enjoyed. The T-Mobile G1 does not.

If your phone does not support multitouch gestures, you can zoom in and out of web pages by tapping the screen to open a small +/− toggle for zooming and shrinking the page. This is a bit of a pain, and not the most efficient way to navigate pages.

Android itself comes with multitouch built into the interface. It's just a matter of whether or not the developers choose to take advantage of it. If you like pinch-to-zoom web browsers and your phone doesn't have one, try downloading the Dolphin browser from the Android market.

Speaker Phone

If your phone came with speaker phone capability, it's fairly simple to use. When you're making a call, you'll see a speaker button. Press the button to activate speaker mode. Press it again to switch to voice. On most phones there's a mute button on the screen as well.

To save batteries, your screen will sleep after a few seconds of inactivity, and phone calls don't count toward that time. If your screen has timed out, tap the trackball to reactivate it.

Security Settings

Now, you could leave your phone as you got it—with no additional security measures. This is the most convenient way to use your phone. However, this means anyone who finds or steals your phone will also have access to your e-mail, your calendar, your call log, and any data you've stored on your phone or connected to your phone through addition apps. It may also be against your workplace security policy.

At a minimum, you should enable a screen lock pattern. As shown in Figure 2–6, Android 2.1 uses a gesture unlocking sequence to enable the screen lock pattern.

1. Go to the Home screen and press the Menu button. Go to Settings ➤ Location & Security ➤ "Set unlock pattern."

2. You'll be shown a series of nine dots. You must connect at least four of them in a continuous motion. Use a gesture you'll remember.

3. Once you've set your pattern, the screen will lock by default, but you'll still be able to use the phone for emergency calls while it's locked.

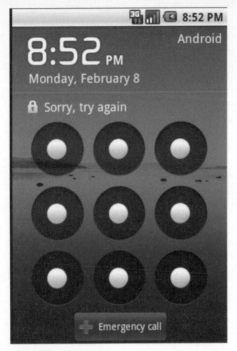

Figure 2–6. *Security*

Android 2.2 also allows you to use a PIN or password in place of a pattern lock.

Another method of security many workplaces insist upon is the remote wipe. Android 2.2 supports remote wiping. You can also purchase third-party software that will do this for you if your phone runs an earlier version of Android. If someone steals your phone, the remote wipe will erase the Exchange data.

> **NOTE:** SMobile Anti-Theft is a $19.95 download that offers remote wipe, antivirus, and GPS location services. It works with most Android phones, but double-check your device compatibility with SMobile before purchasing.

International Settings

The last thing you want to do when traveling internationally is come home to find that you have a thousand-dollar phone bill. Sadly, this has already happened to many a careless traveler that didn't realize they were incurring international roaming charges.

Before you travel, it's important to call your carrier and ask them if they have international data plans and how to arrange them. Theoretically, you can avoid data-roaming charges by turning roaming off before you go. Unless your data plan covers roaming, it's a good idea to turn it off at home, too.

Turn roaming off by going to your Home screen, pressing the Menu button, and then going to Settings ➤ Wireless & Networks ➤ "Mobile networks." Uncheck the box by "Data roaming."

However, other users have reported that they were charged for data access *even after doing this*. This is because third-party apps can override your data settings. If you have an irresponsible app in the background checking for new tweets, you could find yourself with a hefty long-distance bill. You could keep your phone in airplane mode for the entire trip or just leave it at home, but then you won't be able to check for messages or use free Wi-Fi when you are away.

> **NOTE:** APNdroid is a free app that simply turns your data access off by renaming all of your APNs (access point names). This is a simple fix for a vexing problem, and it can even save battery life for times when you're not traveling. Double-check your phone compatibility before installing it. APNdroid does not work with Motorola DROID, and if you choose to uninstall it, make sure you do so when data is *enabled*, or you'll leave yourself stranded with renamed APNs.

Calling Outside the United States

If you are calling an international number from the United States, I encourage you to explore Voice over IP (VoIP) options to make international calls. These use your data plan to make calls instead of using your phone. The prices are generally much better than international cell phone rates, and you can comparison shop to find the best deal. Skype and Google Voice are two popular VoIP options.

You can also download the Calling Card app from the Android Market for using calling cards to route your international calls, including the PIN number. Be sure to specify how you want Calling Card to handle the prefix for international calls.

However, if you do need to dial an international number from within the United States (other than Canada or the Caribbean), be sure to preface each call with 011, followed by the country code, followed by the number. Otherwise, the phone will assume you're making a domestic call prefixed with a 1. Check with your phone carrier to see if it has any alternate requirements for dialing international numbers.

International SIM Cards

If you own an unlocked phone, you might be able to solve your international traveling problems by simply purchasing a prepaid SIM card with data access while abroad. Swap out SIM cards for the duration of the trip. You'll have a different phone number during the trip, but you can still check your e-mail and use maps. You could also check voicemail messages if you have a Google Voice account, although it doesn't support forwarding to international numbers at this time.

Be sure to change your locale settings to reflect your current location.

Summary

Android phones are fairly simple to use once you've acquainted yourself with the basic buttons and motions. Take advantage of the horizontal and vertical orientations for your screen. Once your phone is set up to send and receive e-mail, it's time to start customizing the layout to suit your needs. Take advantage of the multiple pages of Home screen to add apps and shortcuts for easy access to your favorite activities.

Chapter 3

Going Online with Android

Let's face it. You wouldn't be buying a smartphone if you didn't want to go online. Going online doesn't just mean using the built-in web browser in Android. Whether you're using apps or checking your contact list, talking on the phone is just about the only activity that doesn't involve some sort of data plan. That's one of the reasons you can't buy an Android phone without also purchasing a data plan. Trust me, you wouldn't want to try it anyway.

In this chapter, I'll talk about getting online with Android. Android works best when it works online. Google purchased and developed the Android platform with the idea of storing data online or "in the cloud," rather than just on the device. I'll go over the different ways your phone can access data, and how to get the fastest connection with the least amount of battery drain.

Understanding Connection

Back in the days when a car phone meant your phone was built into a car, cell towers actually carried an analog signal, much like a radio signal but at a different frequency. This was the first generation, or 1G, system. The next wave of technology was 2G. Instead of using an analog signal, 2G networks are digital, and most (but not all) carriers started settling on the GSM standard. Verizon and Sprint opted for CDMA instead.

Today most networks offer higher-speed 3G networks of various names, and some are even starting to roll out 4G networks. Once you've selected a phone and a carrier, you don't really need to understand all the technical specs of the various wireless technologies and how they're marketed, but you do need to understand the basics. Other than voice, there are four basic ways your phone connects to signals. Those are Wi-Fi, Bluetooth, GPS, and data.

Wi-Fi

Wi-Fi signals are generally the fastest way to connect to the Internet. This is the same technology that connects laptops and other wireless devices to networks. It's fast but short range, and it's not the same signal they send over cell towers. In order to connect to a Wi-Fi network, you have to be within range of the signal, and you have to be authorized to use the network.

Some bookstores, fast food chains, and restaurants offer free Wi-Fi access networks to anyone within range of the signal. Connecting is easy. Just go to the Android home screen, and then to Settings ➤ Wireless & networks ➤ Wi-Fi settings. Check the boxes to turn on Wi-Fi and receive notification when an open Wi-Fi network is within range.

If you have a Wi-Fi network set up through work or home that is password encrypted, you can use the Wi-Fi settings menu to add the SSID and password to your phone.

The clear advantage to Wi-Fi is speed. You must be connected to Wi-Fi in order to upload video, and watching a video is much faster with Wi-Fi than with the other signals. The disadvantage is distance. Chances are that you're not going to be within range of a Wi-Fi network all day or even most of the day, so whenever you're not within range, you should turn off your Wi-Fi signal in order to save your batteries.

A big consideration with Wi-Fi is security. If you're using an encrypted connection, this isn't as much of a problem, but that convenient, free, open Wi-Fi access point at the coffee shop may in theory expose your phone to unwanted eavesdropping.

Wi-Fi security usually involves some sort of password protection to access the network. An older, less secure method is WEP. If you have a choice in the matter, avoid WEP. It's very easy to crack. A more secure method is WPA or WPA2. Most personal networks, like your router at home, can be set to use WPA-PSK (pre-shared key). This is a fancy way of saying that you have to type in a password or passphrase to get access to the network.

Businesses that want to sell or restrict access to their network use a form of WPA-enterprise. This type of connection usually requires you to log in when you open your first web page, and it compares your username with a list of authorized users. In some cases, you don't actually have to log in, but you do have to click something to agree to the location's terms of service. This is still part of WPA security.

If you aren't required to log into anything, you don't need to click OK to agree to the access rules, and you don't need a password to get onto the network—chances are that you're using an open Wi-Fi access point. A skilled hacker may be able to intercept your signal. Unless you've installed security software, avoid entering passwords or sending sensitive information on open Wi-Fi networks.

Bluetooth

Bluetooth is a super-short-range technology meant as more of a wire replacement than a way to get onto the Internet. Bluetooth can be used to communicate with a wireless headset or your laptop, although Bluetooth file transfer between your phone and a laptop is only supported in Android 2.0 and above. Some apps, like June Fabric's PDANet, also allow you to share your phone's data signal with your laptop using the Bluetooth connection.

For more specific information about Bluetooth, visit the Bluetooth SIG (special interest group) at www.bluetooth.com/.

GPS

GPS stands for Global Positioning System. It's one of the acronyms in this chapter really worth spelling out, because the long name explains what it does. GPS triangulates your position through satellite signals. This isn't the only way your phone can tell where you are, but it's the most common method.

When you use maps or tag your photos by location, the GPS signal is most often used. Android can also supplement this with the location of nearby cell towers and the location of any Wi-Fi networks you're using. However, plenty of apps require a GPS signal to tell you what movies are showing nearby or the location of the nearest Thai restaurant.

GPS activity is represented on the top of your screen as a satellite. If you have GPS activated, you may notice it activating when you open your web browser, even if you aren't doing anything directly map related. This is usually to sense your location for local search results and ads. It's not necessary unless you really do need to find nearby results, so feel free to disable GPS to save battery time.

EDGE, CDMA, and 3G

Connecting to the Internet through Wi-Fi is fast and generally uses less battery life than relying on 3G connections through your phone. However, it's not always available, and one of the best reasons to own a smartphone is so you can get access to the Internet anywhere you happen to be.

Most Android phones can use EDGE and 3G networks. EDGE is also sometimes called 2G, even though it's technically a bit newer than the 2G systems. Using EDGE is like using an old dial-up modem to connect to the Internet. It works, but it's going to be much slower than a 3G connection.

EDGE technology is older and available just about everywhere you can get a phone signal, but newer 3G networks tend to be restricted to high-population areas.

Just to be confusing, Sprint and Verizon have the similar and competing CDMA networks with EVDO technology. The competing technology is different behind the scenes, but CDMA and EDGE look pretty similar on your phone. You will see them labeled as 1x and EV instead of E and 3G.

WiMAX and 4G

The next generation of phone networks are already under construction, but it will still take years before everyone can take advantage of these new high-speed networks. WiMAX is one of the 4G technologies being developed. It's a high-speed, long-distance

Internet signal that can be used for home and phone networks, and will likely be used the same way Wi-Fi is used on smartphones today. Think of it as a form of Wi-Fi that can be broadcast for miles instead of several dozen feet. Sprint and Google are both investors in the WiMAX company Clearwire, so chances are fantastic that Android will be an early adopter of WiMAX.

Unless your phone specifically offers 4G capability, you'll have to buy a new phone to take advantage of WiMAX. Sprint introduced the first 4G Android phone, the HTC EVO. The EVO has an 8-megapixel camera on the back of the phone and a smaller web camera on the front for video conferencing.

Roaming

When you wander outside the range of cell towers that belong to your carrier or have agreements with your carrier, you start roaming. If your carrier charges you for roaming, this can get expensive. In order to avoid accidentally being charged roaming fees, go to the Home screen, and then Settings ➤ Wireless & networks ➤ "Mobile networks." Make sure the box next to "Data roaming" is unchecked. As explained in Chapter 2, some problematic apps might override this setting. You can use APNdroid if necessary. Keep in mind that taking phone calls while roaming may be expensive for your voice plan, too. You may want to shut off the ringer and let all calls go to voicemail until you're back in signal range.

Troubleshooting Connections

The top of your phone will indicate which types of signals you're using and the relative strengths of those signals. You'll also see an up-and-down arrow indicating an active data transfer. There's some variance with the model of phone you use, but most use standard symbols. Figure 3–1 shows a phone that is connected to a 3G network with a relatively weak signal. When data is being transferred over the network, the up-and-down arrow will light up. If you're on a CDMA network like Sprint, you'll see the letters *EV* where the 3G is located.

Figure 3–1. *Top of phone*

Wi-Fi is usually indicated with a dot with curved lines above it to indicate a point giving out signal. GPS is depicted as a satellite. It only shows up when it is actively being used. Bluetooth uses the trademarked Bluetooth symbol.

If you're having trouble with your signal, first check the top of your screen to make sure that you have adequate signal and are using the network you expected to use. If you're using Wi-Fi, make sure you are correctly signed into the network.

Cisco WLC Login

If you log into an enterprise network, such as those used for airports, hospitals, and schools, you may have some difficulty establishing a connection—it depends on how the page is rerouted. This is a known issue with Android's web browser, and as of this publication, it has not been fixed. If you repeatedly get a "page not loaded" error, just use your data plan. It's frustrating, but at least you know it's not just you.

Managing Power

All of this connectivity comes with a cost. In order to save battery power, you should disable services you aren't using. This is especially true when you are traveling and can't charge your phone immediately. Generally, you're going to want to use a 2G signal for passive phone use and making calls. Use 3G when you're surfing the Internet or using data-intensive apps. Keep your GPS off unless you're using a map or other app that hooks into your location. Turn off Wi-Fi and Bluetooth when you're not actively using them.

In order to make all this management easier, some phones ship with a power strip widget that lets you toggle your signal on and off with a touch. If your phone did not ship with one, you can download dozens of widgets to give yourself the same control.

Connecting Securely

As mentioned before, open Wi-Fi networks are not secure. Your phone could be vulnerable to a form of attack known as a man-in-the-middle attack, where someone sitting on the same open network intercepts your unencrypted signal.

Worse yet, anyone can upload an app to the Android store, and that includes malware. The Android Market yanks apps when they're shown to be malicious, but that doesn't mean you can't install a bad app before this happens.

In December 2009, mobile security firm F-Secure reported a suspicious developer named 09Droid making unofficial banking apps. The apps were removed from the Android Market, and several banks issued warnings. However, F-Secure never examined the app itself, so it's entirely possible they were harmless, and F-Secure does have a financial interest in pointing out security flaws on smartphones. It does illustrate the point, though. Downloading an app puts your phone at risk.

To minimize your risk, you should install protection. F-Secure offers browsing protection to identify risky sites, and SMobile offers virus-scanning software. When you download apps, pay attention to the permissions they require.

VPN and SSL

VPNs (virtual private networks) allow you to log into your workplace intranet and enjoy the security of your corporate firewall without having to be hardwired into the network. Some places require this in order to access Exchange e-mail or view sensitive corporate files.

VPNs are natively supported on some but not all Android phones. The Nexus One and Motorola DROID ship with VPN support, but earlier phones like the G1 did not. Android requires hacking for users to be able to log into root access. This is by design. There are apps that allow you to connect with VPN on "rooted" phones, but this should only be attempted if you know what you're doing.

Mocana DSF offers a platform for developers who want to create VPNs and other security tools for Android phones. More information is available at `http://mocana.com/dsf-android.html`. This is geared toward large-scale deployments. If you're just using a personal phone, your best bet is to buy a model that supports VPNs.

If you just need SSL (Secure Socket Layer) for connecting to a web server for file management, you can use ConnectBot. SSL is an Internet standard protocol for transferring information. It's commonly used for transferring files. ConnectBot is available in the Android Market.

To log into a VPN, go to your home screen, press the Menu button, and go to Settings ➤ "Wireless & network settings," as shown in Figure 3–2.

Figure 3–2. *VPN settings*

Next, you'll select VPN settings, as shown in Figure 3–3. If you've already configured a VPN, it will be available here. Otherwise, you'll need to select Add VPN.

Figure 3–3. *Adding a VPN*

The supported choices for Android are shown in Figure 3–4. You'll need to obtain the specific format and settings from your workplace. They include PPTP, L2TP, L2TP/IPSec with PSK, and L2TP/IPSec CRT (certificate based). If your workplace doesn't support one of these protocols, you'll need to work with them to see if there's any other way to log in securely.

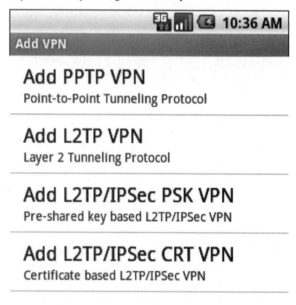

Figure 3–4. *VPN options*

VNC

VNC (Virtual Network Computing) is a way to share screens remotely and control one device from another, even if that device runs on a different platform. If you leave your office or home computer on at all times and your office allows it, you can use VNC to check documents, send e-mail, or execute work tasks from wherever you are. VNC can be used with Mac, Windows, and Linux computers.

In order to use VNC securely, it should also be paired with a VPN. There are several VNC clients available for Android, including Android VNC Viewer, Remote VNC, and PhoneMyPC.

Right now Android isn't a large target, but as the number of devices on the market will expand, so will the number of hackers targeting Android. The open OS gives anyone who wishes a glimpse of the code. That gives users a chance to patch flaws, but it also gives hackers a chance to find and exploit them. Android was built with security in mind, but some of that security relies on you. Apps are only allowed limited privileges. As you install apps from the Android Market, pay attention to the permissions you are granting. I'll cover this in more detail in Chapter 14.

Android's Web Browser

Now that I've discussed the various ways Android phones can connect to data, let's talk about surfing the Web. Android has a full-featured web browser based on WebKit. This is the same base for the Chrome and Safari web browsers. Generally, it behaves the same as most web browsers. You can also download alternative browsers like Dolphin or Opera.

One thing to note is that the Android browser is *not* Internet Explorer. You may encounter sites that absolutely will not work unless you use Internet Explorer. You may also encounter web sites that won't work without plug-ins and extensions that aren't available on Android. If you find this is the case, you might be able to get around it by using VNC and launching Internet Explorer from your remote computer.

Basic Web Navigation

Some Android variations have some slight differences in how their web browsers work, but they will all browse the Web. To launch the Android browser, just click the Browser app. By default, you'll see the Google home page, as shown in Figure 3–5. Some phone manufacturers may change the default home screen in favor of something else. You can change your default screen by long-clicking a bookmark. I'll explain this more soon.

You can search for a site in the search box, or click the URL box to enter a new address. Some web pages display in a mobile-friendly format, but some are just regular web pages. You can make the tiny type displayed by them larger either by using the pinch-to-zoom motion (available on some phones) or by tapping the screen and using the + and – buttons to adjust the screen size.

Figure 3–5. *Android web browser*

Using Bookmarks

If you do any sort of serious web surfing, you'll want to save some bookmarks. Figure 3–5 shows the Android web browser in Android 2.1. Next to the URL box, you'll see a star button that allows you to save the site as a bookmark. Clicking that button will bring up the screen shown in Figure 3–6.

This is a very handy bookmark browser. It comes prepopulated with some common sites, but you can add your own. You can also use the tabs at the top to find sites by your browsing history or by the sites you view most often.

You don't need to add a bookmark to see this menu. You can get back to this bookmark browser by clicking the Menu button while browsing a web page.

Figure 3–6. *Bookmarks*

Adding Shortcuts to Your Home Screen

If you use a site regularly, it makes a lot of sense to put a one-stop bookmark on your Home screen. To add a shortcut, just go to the bookmark browser and long-click your desired bookmark. As shown in Figure 3–7, this will pull up a screen that lets you set a bookmark as your browser's home page or add a shortcut to the Home screen (Add shortcut to Home).

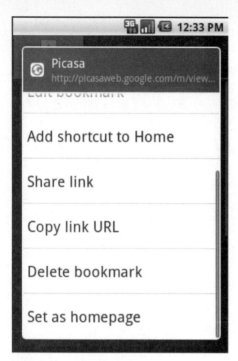

Figure 3–7. *Adding a shortcut*

Navigating Multiple Pages

There's not enough room on a phone to have tabs for multiple sites like you would on a desktop browser. If you've got more than one page open or you want to open more windows, click the Menu button within the Browser app and then click Windows. You'll see a list of all the currently available windows and the option to add more.

Once you're done with a window, you'll want to shut it down to conserve memory. Use the same Windows button to remove extra open windows by clicking the X next to the window you want to close.

Adobe announced in February 2010 that they were also developing Flash for Android along with other mobile devices like BlackBerry, Palm, and Windows Mobile. (Yes, the iPhone is missing from that list.) Although Flash is a common Internet plug-in for rich content like games and video, it wasn't supported on mobile devices, which means many streaming video sites and popular Internet games haven't been able to work on phones. Flash is currently available as a download for phones running Android 2.2 and higher.

Summary

Going online with Android is so easy that it takes effort to not be online. Android devices can connect to data using GPS, Wi-Fi, Bluetooth, and cellular data technologies. Use the symbols at the top of the screen to tell when you're connected, and turn off data sources you're not using to save power.

You can also use Android with a VPN network to take advantage of your workplace intranet or VNC to control devices remotely.

The Android web browser is a fully functional browser that will let you manage bookmarks and navigate multiple pages, but using an open Wi-Fi network may be risky, so you should install browser security software and be mindful when you download apps.

Chapter 4

Android Calling

Android phones are amazing small computing devices that can connect you to the Internet just about anywhere, but they are also phones. In this chapter, you'll explore the phone features of Android and get to the nitty-gritty of sending and receiving calls and managing your contacts.

You'll also look at Google Voice as a VoIP option for forwarding calls and using visual voicemail.

Using the Dialer

The first time my husband tried to make a call with his Android phone, he tried browsing to the dialer app in the app tray and then making the call. It works, but it involves a lot of unnecessary extra steps. He could have just pushed the green button on the phone.

The dialer is the built-in app responsible for dialing the phone, browsing your contacts, and keeping a log of calls you've received. If your phone doesn't come with a button that launches it directly, there's usually a shortcut to the dialer on your Home screen.

Dialer App Anatomy

Figure 4–1 shows the four basic areas of the dialer app: Phone, Call log, Contacts, and Favorites. Some phones have variations on the look and feel of these areas, but the basic layout is pretty consistent.

Figure 4–1. *The dialer app*

Calling

If you want to make a call using the dialer, you just use the number pad to dial your number and then press the phone icon to the left of your number. The back arrow with the X in it will delete the last digit. On earlier versions of Android, this back arrow was near the top of the screen, next to the number, and the green phone was on the left. I don't know how many times I started deleting numbers instead of pressing the call button. Thankfully, the green Call button and Delete button are more distinct, and are at the bottom of the screen for phones using Android 2.1 and 2.2.

As you're calling, the screen will black out to save energy. If you need to see the screen again, such as when you need to press numbers to navigate a voicemail system, just tap the trackball to wake up the screen.

Red means stop, so if the background turns red, the phone call has ended. You can also hit the red phone button to end the call yourself.

Browsing Call History

As shown in Figure 4–2, the call log lets you view the history of your recent phone calls. You can see the name and number of the caller, whether or not you answered the call, and whether or not the caller left a voicemail message. You can also click the green phone button next to the entry to dial that number again.

Figure 4–2. *The call log*

Android's call log is pretty standard. If you've used a cell phone, this isn't new territory.

If you want to delete your call log, you can do so by pressing the Menu button and selecting the appropriate option. A periodic purge may be a good habit if you deal with patients or clients and want to keep your conversations confidential.

Managing Your Contacts

Over the years, I've had PDAs, phones, calendar programs, and e-mail addresses—all with a different set of contacts. Managing all those contacts gets complicated, so it's a big relief to merge them into a single contact list I can use on my phone or the Web.

Android syncs your contact list with Google Contacts. This is the same place Gmail gets its information. You can manage your contacts either on your phone or on the Web, but for major changes, it's easier to manage everything on the Web and enjoy a full keyboard.

Figure 4–3 shows Google Contacts (at www.google.com/contacts). The only caveat about using Google Contacts is that not all of its features are supported on the phone. If you create a group, it won't show up as a group in your phone's contact list.

However, the web interface is super-handy for merging all those inevitable duplicates. You can search automatically by using the Find Duplicates button on the right. You can also merge contacts by selecting the check box next to two or more contacts and selecting the Merge option. Merged contacts combine all the additional phone numbers and addresses, but be sure to double-check that the correct name has been picked for the contact.

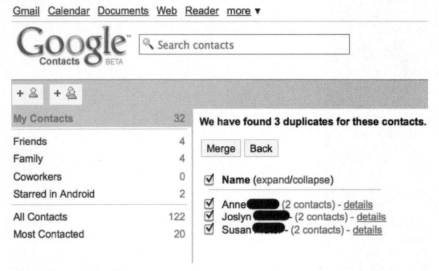

Figure 4–3. *Google Contacts*

> **TIP:** Browse quickly through your contact list, and you'll see a pop-up letter in the middle of the screen. This is the letter of the alphabet you're scrolling past, so you can get to your desired contact quickly.

Adding Contacts on Your Phone

Although I'm a big fan of using the web interface when possible, it's just not practical to enter every phone number that way. When you're out and about with your phone, you can add contacts by using the Menu button from within your contacts and selecting New Contact.

You can enter as much or as little as you wish. Pressing the green + next to a detail will add more detail items (e.g., you can add more phone numbers or e-mail addresses). You can also break these down to differentiate between work, home, and cell numbers within a single contact.

Pressing the red – will delete an item. Use this to rid yourself of outdated e-mail addresses. Press the empty gray square where the picture should be, and you can use any picture on your phone's memory. You can also take a quick photo of your contact to include.

Press the More button to add helpful things like notes and nicknames. I like to add nearby landmarks for finding addresses and likes/dislikes for buying gifts.

You can use a similar process to edit contacts. Just press the Menu button while viewing the contact details and select Edit. You can also get there by long-clicking a name in the contact list. You'll see a screen like Figure 4–4, which lets you change your contact details.

Figure 4–4. *Adding contacts*

Deleting Contacts

If you need to delete a contact, just press the Menu button while viewing the contact details, and select the "Delete contact" option. You'll get a confirmation dialog, and, once you confirm, your contact will be deleted on both your phone and the Web.

Favorites

Use your favorites list to keep track of special numbers. Your favorites list contains the numbers you've specifically designated as favorites at the top, and the numbers you call the most frequently underneath. Add contacts to your favorites by pressing the star next to their name when viewing the contact details. Press the star again to remove them.

Personalizing Contacts

You can't add your phone numbers into groups the way you can in Google Contacts, and there's only so many favorites you can track before that becomes unmanageable, too. You can add more memory aids to help you track your contacts and put them in context.

Customizing Ringtones

One of the easiest ways to tell who is calling is to give them a custom ringtone. To do this, follow these steps:

1. First, browse to the contact and select it.

2. While viewing the contact, press the Menu button.

3. Select Options. Click the Ringtones button, as shown in Figure 4–5.

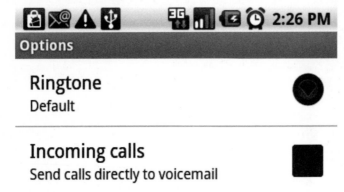

Figure 4–5. *Custom ringtones*

4. Select the desired ringtone.

It's going to make noise when you select each ringtone, so either mute the volume first or set it up where noise isn't a problem.

Pictures

Some of your contacts are going to come with pictures without your having to do any extra work; these pictures may come from Facebook or Google profiles. However, not everyone will have a picture already associated with their name. You don't need a picture to go with every contact, but sometimes it's nice to put a face with a name.

As mentioned earlier, when editing a contact, you can click the gray default picture and insert any picture you have stored on your phone. You can also snap a picture on the spot. Pictures will display when making or receiving calls or browsing your contact list.

Shortcuts

You can add shortcuts to just about anything to the home screen, including contacts. Just long-click the Home screen and select "Shortcuts." You'll see a list of shortcuts that includes three types of contact options, as shown in Figure 4–6. Those options are direct dial, direct message, and contact.

Figure 4–6. *Shortcuts*

Direct dial and direct message do what they imply, and immediately call or SMS message your contact with the specific number you've selected. Adding the contact option (the middle shortcut in Figure 4–6) is the most versatile.

Click once on the contact, and you'll see small icons for quick navigation to phone, message, Facebook, and the full contact file. These shortcuts are contained in a local, private database.

Folders

Add as many contacts to your Home screen as will fit. But why stop there? Instead of adding a single contact, you can add a folder. To do this, long-click the Home screen and select Folder. You'll be presented with several choices for including contacts, such as all contacts, contacts with phone numbers, starred contacts, and Facebook phone numbers. You can also add a blank folder.

You can move items into blank folders by long-clicking them and then dragging. Rename a folder by clicking the folder name. Be aware that removing a folder from your Home screen also removes its contents.

> **TIP:** This phone OS was made by Google, so of course it searches! Rather than trying to browse through long lists of contacts, you can press the quick-search button at any time. If you're within the dialer app, your search will show you only contacts. If you're searching from the Home screen, search results will include "Web" and "contacts." Note that this quick-search box, which appears when you press the physical button, is different from the *web*-specific search widget on your Home screen.

Voicemail Basics

Android doesn't come with a fantastic voicemail app built in. That's because voicemail depends a lot on your carrier and its system. There are some settings on your contact page to let you dial into your carrier's voicemail system, but it's still not visual voicemail.

Visual Voicemail

Rather than navigating the voice options by listening and pressing buttons, visual voicemail gives you the option of viewing voicemail messages like you would your calling history. You can browse through your messages and then listen once you've found a message of interest. Your phone carrier may offer a free visual voicemail app, or you can use Google Voice as your visual voicemail solution. Usually, visual voicemail apps come preinstalled, but if you purchase a Nexus One, check with your carrier. I'll discuss Google Voice in more detail in a bit.

Straight to Voicemail

If you've got a very nice but long-winded contact that seems to always call at the wrong time, one way to deal with it is to send all of their calls straight to voicemail. When viewing their contact page, click the Menu button, select options, and then check the appropriate box.

To Google Voice or Not to Google Voice

I love Google Voice. It's a free service from Google that forwards calls through VoIP. You can create a phone number that will forward to one or more of your phones. I use mine to call both my husband and my phones, since one of us is usually available to answer that way.

If you change phones, no problem. Just forward to your new number. Temporary number? Again, not a problem. You can also search for available numbers by letter or number combination, so you'll have a single point of contact that you can remember.

Google Voice is also available as a phone app. You can use your phone as if your Google Voice number were your only phone number. Outgoing calls would list your Google Voice number in the caller ID info. That's pretty powerful, but you don't have to use it this way. You can use all or part of the services and toggle them on or off at will, as illustrated in Figure 4–7.

You can also use Google Voice without getting a new number, though you'll be severely limited in the features available if you do it that way.

Figure 4–7. *Google Voice*

How to Get a Google Voice Account

Previously Google Voice required an invitation, but now the service is open to anyone in the United States. Sign up for an account at www.google.com/voice.

Once you've set up your Google Voice account on the Web, download the Google Voice app from the Android Market. Once you've installed it, you can choose to use Google Voice for all or none of your calls, or have Google Voice ask every time. This dialog is shown in Figure 4–7.

Selecting a Google Voice Phone Number

Once you register, you should pick a number. You can search through available numbers by number or letter to find something meaningful. While you can restrict this to only your area code, it's not a requirement. Most people seem to use cell phones for long distance, and cell phones don't care what area code you have.

Using Your Own Phone Number

If you choose, you can avoid getting a new number for Google Voice and just use the number from your cell phone. However, if you do this, you can't forward any calls to different numbers. It's only good for the phone you use. You're basically limited to voicemail transcription and international calls.

Free Text Messages

If you install the Google Voice app on your phone, you can choose to use your Google Voice number in place of your regular number for SMS text messages. If your phone didn't come with a text plan, you've just created one, and this one is free.

Visual Voicemail and Transcription

Google Voice also comes with its own visual voicemail interface, as shown in Figure 4–8. So long as people call your Google Voice number, messages are stored in the Google Voice inbox. Better yet, it transcribes them, so you can sort through messages as if they were e-mails.

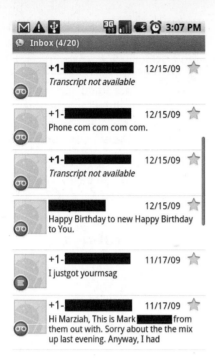

Figure 4–8. *Google Voice inbox*

It's far from perfect. You still get garbled words, but it gives you a good idea what the message says before you need to put the phone to your ear, and it gets better with practice. You can also have your Google Voice messages sent to you by text or e-mail.

International Calling

You can't use Google Voice to forward your calls to phones outside the United States, but you can use your Google Voice account to make cheap international long-distance calls. You do this by loading credits to your Google Voice account through Google Checkout. Do this through the Google Voice web site by clicking the Add Credit link. You can add credits in increments of $10. Google greases the wheel to get you started by giving you a $1 credit.

Conference Calls

If you have call forwarding, you can take advantage of free conference calls for up to four people if your phone service comes with call waiting. Just have everyone call you on your Google Voice number, and Google will give you the option to conference the new calls as they arrive. Typically, you'd just press 5 on the keypad when you hear the vocal instructions.

Personalized Actions

Remember those groups from Google Contacts that weren't useful in your dialer? They're useful here. If you go to the Google Voice web interface at www.google.com/voice, you can change how your calls forward for individual numbers or for contact groups. Go to Settings at the upper right of the screen and then navigate to the Groups tab. Family members could ring your home phone while business colleagues ring your work phone. Your spouse could ring all your numbers, and your neighbor could go straight to voicemail.

You can also block numbers from calling you completely. In this case, the caller will hear a recording of "This number is no longer in service" instead.

Toggling Between Google Voice and Your Cell Number

Rather than being locked to your Google Voice number for all inbound and outbound calls, you can toggle the features on and off at will. If you've got the Google Voice app installed on the phone, you can also install a toggle widget. Long-click your Home screen to find this option.

Disadvantages of Using Google Voice

Transcribed Google Voice messages may pose a security risk for some businesses, and if they're sent to your work e-mail, they're subject to data retention laws the same as every other e-mail. Check with your employer on how you should handle this. They may prefer that you do not e-mail transcriptions, or they may prefer that you do not generate transcriptions in the first place.

The other big drawback with Google Voice is that it doesn't support dialing numbers with extensions. That means you can't use it full time for outbound calls to most business numbers. Either toggle Google Voice off using the toggle widget or don't use it as your default number.

Summary

Android phones have powerful features to let you manage your contacts and personalize your phone experience. Contacts added in Android are backed up on the Web with Google Contacts. Take advantage of Home screen shortcuts and folders to organize frequently called contacts. Sign up for a Google Voice account for powerful phone-forwarding options and free SMS text messaging.

Chapter **5**

Managing Texting

SMS stands for Short Message Service, but most of the time it's just referred to as *texting*. The first text was sent in 1992, but the standard for text messages was developed as early as 1985. The message "Merry Christmas" marked the beginning of non-voice services on phones.

Text messages can be very valuable to the productive worker. Sign up for messages if your flight is canceled. Use messages to alert your customers of a change in plans or to give customer service and resolve a problem. Request follow-up information during a meeting without having to interrupt the meeting to make a voice call. Send pictures of a job site from the field.

In this chapter, we'll cover sending and receiving text messages, using alternatives to text messages, and using apps to extend your texting abilities.

Texting Basics

SMS text messages are *short* messages. The limit is 160 or 140 characters, depending on the phone and the application sending the message. Why so short? It's an old standard, and the technology at the time wouldn't have supported long essays. According to the *Los Angeles Times*, one of the standard's developers, Friedhelm Hillebrand, determined that 160 characters was long enough for short messages based on his own writing.

Texting took off, in part because an early billing loophole made texts cheaper than voice minutes. The wrinkles in billing have long since been ironed out, but texting remains popular. It's also moved beyond teens chatting with each other.

SMS messages also evolved into allowing MMS (Multimedia Messaging Service) messages. MMS messages, or "picture messages," are a popular way to share pictures taken on a phone, but they can also be used to share video and other formats.

Before you delve into texting, you better understand how much this will cost. The trend for smartphones, including Android, is to bundle the phone with a plan that includes unlimited data and unlimited text. However, you may have a legacy plan that doesn't include text.

Check your phone plan to see how many text messages you're allotted each month. You'll also want to ask if your network supports MMS under that plan, and you'll want to find out how much it costs to text while roaming. Finally, check the price of sending or receiving international texts. You may not intend to text someone in the United Kingdom next week, but it doesn't hurt to know how much it will cost in advance.

Keep in mind also that unlimited texting does not mean that premium texting is also included. If you text to vote for the next reality TV star or text a charitable donation, you will still be expected to pay for it, even if your plan includes unlimited texts.

> **NOTE:** Android developers will be happy to know that they don't need a device with a text plan in order to test SMS messaging. The Android desktop emulator sends text from the computer.

Sending

Texting capability is built into Android and integrated into all the services. There is a standalone Messaging app you can use, or you can launch a text session from your contacts list in the dialer app. If you're using a phone with Android 2.0 or higher, just click the picture of a contact (not the name), and you'll see what looks like a bubble quote and symbols representing the way you can send a message to that contact, as shown in Figure 5–1. The messaging symbol in pure Android 2.2 looks like a quote bubble with a smiley face.

In Android 1.6 phones like the G1, you can't use this method. There are no pictures in the contact list. Instead, you click the name of the contact and choose either to phone or text message. The symbol for text messaging in Android 1.6 is also different. It looks like a small postcard. Other user interface overlays have different symbols. The HTC Hero messaging symbol looks like a postcard in a quote bubble, for example.

You can also send messages directly from the Messaging app. Start typing a name from your contact list or enter a phone number directly. You can also enter multiple contact names or phone numbers to send a message to a group. Type in your message, and press Send.

If you happen to enter a dead zone while you're texting, your message will be sent when you regain the signal.

Figure 5–1. *Selecting messaging from your contact list*

Autocomplete

Phones without keyboards send messages entirely through the number pad.

Android phones all have either a physical or virtual keyboard, so you won't have to deal with how many times to press numbers. They also make suggestions as you type. Figure 5–2 shows a word suggestion. If one of the words being suggested matches the word you're typing, tap the word, and it will be completed for you. The phone's vocabulary expands as you go. My phone started suggesting "Marziah" to m-a-r words after a couple weeks of use.

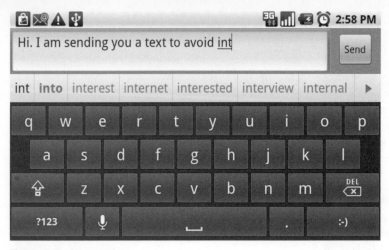

Figure 5–2. *Autocomplete*

Receiving

When you receive a new text, depending on your notification settings, you'll get the "notification" ringtone. This can be different from the ringtone you get for incoming calls. I have my notification ringtone set to silent. You'll also see a notification at the top of the screen showing you have a new message. The symbol will depend on the phone and version of Android, but it will be the same symbol used for your Messaging app.

Swipe your finger from the top of the screen downward to pull down the notification tab. You'll see the message, and if you need to respond, click directly on the messaging symbol to open the Messaging app. You can also just launch the Messaging app from the home screen.

Links and numbers within SMS messages are generally clickable. Android is interpreting links behind the scenes. Sometimes Android goes slightly too far and will make any random string of numbers clickable, even when it isn't a phone number.

> **TIP:** By default in Android 2.2, there's no fancy pop-up window to let you know you've received a text message, but you can install an app like SMS Popup if you want a more intrusive alert when you get new messages.

Forwarding

If you want to forward a message to someone else, just long-click the message and select Forward from the options. You can also use the Options menu to copy the message text in case you'd like to send the message by e-mail, or copy it to a note or onto a map.

Multimedia and MMS

You can send attachments like pictures, videos, and audio files through MMS. You use the Messaging app for this. While composing a message, just press the Menu button and select the Attach option. Browse through the options for the type of media you'd like to attach, as shown in Figure 5–3.

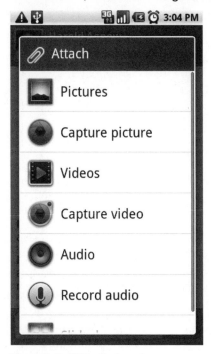

Figure 5–3. *MMS attachments*

Settings

From within the Messaging app, press the Menu button and select Settings, as shown in Figure 5–4. You have several options to control how you manage your messages, including how your messages are stored and when you automatically delete old ones.

If it's vital that your recipient read the message, you can use the "Read reports" and "Delivery reports" options. Unfortunately, as of Android 2.1, read reports don't work reliably, so ask for confirmation directly from the recipient instead. You can also use the app chompSMS, which supports the feature.

An option toward the bottom of the screen that you should definitely watch is "Roaming auto-retrieve." It's off by default, and on most phones it should remain that way. When this is on, your phone will still try to retrieve messages while you're roaming, and that could mean a roaming charge on your phone bill.

Figure 5–4. *Message settings*

Going Beyond the Defaults

The SMS standard is pretty old. It's handy because it's a standard, but there are plenty of other ways to send non-voice messages on smartphones, and a lot of them may make more sense with the way you use your phone.

You also may want features that just aren't supported by the default Messaging app. This section will explore alternatives to SMS text messaging, like instant messaging (IM), and look at ways to use your data plan to send SMS messages.

Texting vs. IM

In a lot of practical uses, text messages are just like instant messages. So, if you and the recipient both have an IM client, it makes a lot of sense to just keep the conversation on IM. Android phones come with Google Talk for IM, but you can install apps to handle most other clients. Unfortunately, Microsoft Office Communicator is not yet one of them, but that may change at any time.

Instant messages use your data plan instead of your text plan. Many of them support multimedia attachments, and you can extend your availability by having an IM client installed on your computer. You can also send instant messages to someone internationally without having to pay higher fees, since it's all just data transmission.

Google Voice

Last chapter, I talked about Google Voice. One of the options in Google Voice is the ability to send and receive SMS text messages, as shown in Figure 5–5. This gets around your texting plan and uses your data service instead. However, there are some caveats. As I'm writing this, Google Voice doesn't support MMS messages, international messages, or receiving "short-code" messages. (These are messages sent by services like Twitter that use a shorter number for dialing.)

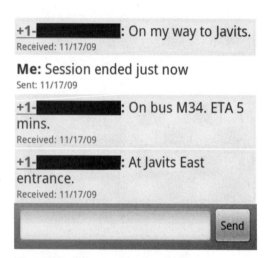

Figure 5–5. *Messages from Google Voice*

You can, however, use Google Voice in tandem with your SMS plan. Use the Messaging app when you need to send an MMS message, and use Google Voice for other messages.

chompSMS

If you like the iPhone quote-bubble look, you can use chompSMS, a free app that emulates that. You can also use chompSMS to send reduced-rate international texts through the chompSMS network. chompSMS also supports read receipts—so fixing that bug alone may make it worth installing.

Other nice features with chompSMS include the ability to send texts to a group at a time instead of having to enter each address individually. You can also use it to blacklist senders like spammers or marketing firms.

SMS Gateway and Outlook

One of the specifications of SMS text messages is that you can send them from phone to phone, and also from computer to phone. SMS gateway services provide computer-to-phone and phone-to-computer services. SMS gateway services make it possible for you to sign up for SMS updates from web sites.

Outlook Mobile Service (OMS) is an extension of Outlook 2007 that can forward e-mail, tasks, and events to your phone. You can use it to forward important messages, send yourself task reminders, or send messages to coworkers on the road.

It's not free, and to use it you need to sign up with a hosting provider specific to your carrier. For more information, visit Microsoft's page on OMS, at `http://office.microsoft.com/en-us/outlook/HA101078921033.aspx`.

> **NOTE:** Some web sites also provide free SMS gateway service for personal messages in the hope that you'll become an eventual business customer. SMS Everywhere (http://smseverywhere.com/) is one example.

Twitter and Texting

Twitter is a service that was developed and built around the idea of texting. Twitter users "microblog" in messages that are 140 characters or less. Text messages can be 160 characters long, but in Twitter those extra 20 characters are used to identify the sender.

If you have a Twitter account, you can enter your phone number to get text notifications for direct messages, or *tweets*, from specific people. You can also text to Twitter in order to create messages.

There are better and easier-to-use apps for using Twitter, so unless you're unable to install apps on your phone, there's no compelling reason to use Twitter by SMS.

Texting for Charity

You can send charity donations through text by texting a specific message to a specific five-digit number. This is another use of short-code numbers. Carriers and companies have agreements that allow the carrier to be charged for the text, and the carrier then passes the fee on to you at the next billing cycle.

The advantage is that you can quickly and easily donate or raise money for a cause. The disadvantage is that the charities pay a fee in order to be able to receive donations this way, and the money will be delayed because it's not collected until you get your phone bill. However, the amount of money that can be raised this way is truly impressive. One example of the power of this effort was shown when the Red Cross set up an SMS donation site for earthquake victims in Haiti, and raised more than $30 million for their cause from $10 donations.

If you're curious to see how you can donate or set up a charitable SMS fundraiser for your own cause, here are some companies that offer the service:

- `http://www.mgive.com/`
- `http://www.mobilecommons.com/`
- `http://www.mobilegiving.org/`
- `http://wirelessfactory.com/us/mdonation`
- `https://xipwirer.com/`

Texting Google

Google will actually answer search questions by SMS. If you text 466453 (the numbers spell out "Google") you can ask a search question and receive a text answer. It's especially handy for finding things nearby. Good examples are things like "movies Chicago, IL" or "weather Detroit." You can also get quick answers to things like "cups in ounces."

The answers are completely automated, but they don't cost you anything beyond what you pay your carrier for regular text messages.

GOOG 411

In addition to texting Google, you can also call them. If you dial GOOG 411 (1-800-466-4411) from any phone, you can get local search results. Use this to find a nearby business or landmarks.

Once you have your results, you can say "Text it," and Google will send you a text message with the address, or "Map it," and you'll receive a text with a link to map directions. This is handy during cold weather when you don't want to get your hands out to dial or enter map locations.

Voice to Text

If you have a phone that supports voice entry, like the HTC EVO, you can send text messages without having to type anything. Voice to Text is a paid app that provides the same features for other phones. Speech recognition technology isn't always the most accurate, so buyer beware.

Texting and Security

SMS is an old standard, so it's vulnerable to new tricks. An iPhone vulnerability in 2009 posed a risk to a potentially large number of phones, and there isn't any guarantee that someone won't find a vulnerability in Android.

In addition, SMS is not encrypted and not a recommended way to send sensitive data. You may be able to add some encryption using third-party apps, but e-mail and password-protected web sites are probably a safer bet. Check with your workplace to see what their policy is for business-related SMS.

Summary

Text messaging has moved beyond teenagers chatting and can be used for serious business. It can be used to keep customers satisfied and yourself organized. It can be used to communicate with one or many people. You can install apps to extend your text capabilities with Android as well. However, it's important to know how much texting services will cost you, and it's good to know when you can rely on an alternative like e-mail or IM.

Chapter 6

Wrangling Your E-mail

One of the big reasons to have a smartphone is to keep on top of your e-mail. If you're using an older version of Android (1.5 or 1.6), you're stuck with one account per e-mail app. If you're using Android 2.0 or later, you've got more options. There are also variations for phones that came with custom Android user interfaces and options.

With standard Android phones, there are basically four options for e-mail:

- The Gmail app
- The Email app
- The Android web browser
- Third-party apps

Figure 6–1 shows several typical apps you can use to access e-mail. In this chapter, you'll get to know those options and how you can send, receive, and manage your e-mail. You'll learn more about Gmail and how to use it effectively. I'll go into more detail about syncing and managing Exchange accounts with your Android device as well.

Figure 6–1. *E-mail options*

Getting to Know Gmail

Gmail is the default e-mail app for Android phones, unless the default was modified by the device maker or carrier. In order to understand Gmail's mobile version, it's helpful to first understand Gmail on the Web. You'll also need to visit Gmail on the Web in order to get the best use of Gmail by setting up filters and experimenting with new features.

Gmail is arguably the best free e-mail service available. There's no automatic tagline on the end of your messages advertising that you're using a free e-mail. You don't have to pay extra in order to use a desktop or mobile app to access your e-mail. The spam filtering is above average, and you get plenty of storage space. In fact, Gmail works so well that many business users have come to rely on the service through the enterprise Google Apps suite.

> **NOTE:** Although it's not a faux pas to use a Gmail address for professional correspondence, you can use Google Apps to send and receive Gmail through custom business URLs. If you own a small or medium-sized business, you can take advantage of Google's services from either the limited, free, "standard" account, or the $50-per-user-per-year "premium" account. If you're the sole owner of your business or a consultant, you could use Google Apps as a free e-mail service for a domain name you already own. For more information, visit Google Apps at www.google.com/a.

Inbox and Archive

Gmail doesn't have folders. Instead of folders, Gmail uses labels. I'll get to that next—but let's just say that, for most purposes, there are only two places for e-mail you want to keep: the inbox and the archive.

There are two places for e-mail you don't want to keep: trash and spam. Generally, you'll want to mark spammy messages appropriately before deleting them, because this helps train the spam filters to recognize unwanted messages.

If you don't ever want a message again, by all means delete it. E-mail sent to the trash is permanently deleted after 30 days. However, messages you might need later should be archived. To archive a message from the Web, select the check box next to the message, and then click the Archive button (on left side of the buttons above the inbox, as shown in Figure 6–2).

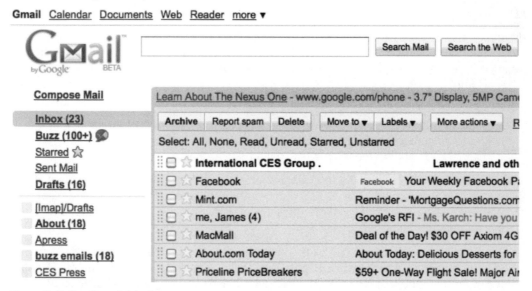

Figure 6–2. *Gmail's web interface*

When you archive a message, you move it out of the inbox. You can still find the message by using the All Mail label or by using the Gmail search box. For messages of low importance, you may even want to set up a filter that archives the messages immediately so they never clog your inbox. I'll explain how to do that later in this chapter.

NOTE: Gmail messages are grouped into conversations. Rather than showing each message in the order they arrived, conversations are clusters of messages to and from a person or group. The messages are stacked together, so you can view the conversation in context, and they appear chronologically in your inbox according to the last message received. Any actions you apply to one message in the conversation will apply to all of them. If you want to view or act on the messages individually, just click the "Expand all" link to the right of the message. If you keep seeing a super-long conversation that you'd rather ignore, use the Mute option to archive the current and future messages in that conversation. The messages will still be available and marked as unread. They just won't be in your inbox.

Labels

Many e-mail accounts work by allowing you to place e-mail messages in folders. Gmail would prefer you use labels. What is the difference? A single piece of e-mail can only exist in a single folder; you'd have to copy an e-mail message for it to be both in the "Work" and "Tax-Related" folders. On the other hand, a single e-mail can have multiple labels.

Use labels to organize your messages by topic. You can click one of the labels on the left side of the screen (as shown in Figure 6–2) to view only messages with that particular label, including messages that have been archived.

Gmail automatically creates the following labels: Inbox, Buzz, Starred, Chats, Sent Mail, Drafts, All Mail, Spam, and Trash. You can create other labels as needed. I often set up temporary labels for upcoming conferences or events and then remove or hide the labels after the conference.

Notice the Starred label. You can click the star to the left of a message in order to mark it with the star label, which just highlights the message with a yellow star. Since you can apply more than one label to an item, adding both a star and a different label could emphasize urgent messages or highlight items that need a response or require action.

Creating and Deleting Labels

You can create labels many ways. If you click the Labels button at the top of your inbox and then click "Manage labels" from the drop-down menu, you enter the label settings area. You can enter new labels by typing into the box labeled "Create a new label." You can also get to this menu by clicking the Settings link at the upper right of the screen and then clicking Labels. Another method is to click the More link at the bottom of your label list on the left side of the screen. It might have a number in front of it if you have a lot of labels already (e.g., "10 more").

You're limited to 40 characters for label names, but it would be wise to keep them even shorter. Long labels mean less space for your message previews.

You can edit a label by clicking the label name in the label settings and then typing the new name in. You can show or hide labels by clicking the link to the right of the labels, and you can delete them as well. Deleting a label does not delete the messages.

Automatic Filters

Automatic filters are probably one of the most powerful tools in any e-mail program. When combined with labels, Gmail lets you do quite a lot with filters. To get started, simply click the check box next to one or more messages and then click the "More actions" button. Select "Filter messages like these."

Gmail will try to guess the criteria you're using, such as messages from a certain sender or messages containing a particular subject line. If the guess is wrong, you can change the criteria. Once you've got the correct criteria, click the Next Step button.

Now you choose an action. Your choices include archive (the Skip the Inbox option), star, mark as read, apply a label, forward, delete, and never flag as spam. You can select more than one action for an item, such as starring and never marking it as spam.

Next, create the filter. You can also select the check box to apply that filter to any previous messages that matched your criteria.

I use filters to automatically prioritize messages from business contacts with stars and subject labels. I declutter by archiving distracting mailing lists I may want to read later and notifications from Facebook and Twitter. I also make sure important senders never have their messages marked as spam.

> **NOTE:** You can create an easy filter for a group or project by creating a custom e-mail address. Your Gmail address supports adding words to your address by adding them on with a + sign. For instance, you can have everyone involved with a project send messages to YourUserName+YourProject@gmail.com. You can add a filter for messages sent to that specific address, and then apply the desired label.

The Settings Menu

We've already explored filters and labels, but there are many other options on the Settings menu worth mentioning. To adjust settings, click the Settings link at the upper right of the Gmail web screen, just next to your e-mail address.

General Settings

The first tab offers some general settings. Make sure your browser connection is set to "Always use https://." That ensures that you'll use a more secure connection to check your e-mail when using a web browser. It's also the default setting, so if you don't have either one selected, it's still using the secure connection.

The other important things to note are that you can create text signatures and set automatic vacation replies through the appropriate boxes here. Be aware that any signatures you create here will *not* translate to your phone. You have to set those up separately.

If you change anything, be sure to click the Save Changes button before moving on.

Accounts

You can add additional e-mail accounts through Gmail and check and respond to them from the same inbox as your Gmail account. They have to be standard POP3 accounts, but that includes most web-based e-mail and e-mail accounts offered through Internet service providers (ISPs). That generally does not include Exchange accounts.

If you add accounts, you'll want to decide if you should respond from the address that received the e-mail or always use your default e-mail address. I find it less confusing to respond with the same account that originated the e-mail. Your default address is the address you'll use to compose new messages.

If you're using Android 2.0 or higher, you can also add more Gmail accounts from your phone, but if you're using Android 1.6, you'll want to add them here.

Forwarding and POP/IMAP

You can automatically forward a copy of each message to a different account and either keep, archive, or delete the original message. This applies to *all* messages to that account, but you can forward selectively by creating a filter.

For accessing e-mail on your Android phone, you'll want to enable IMAP (Internet Message Access Protocol). This is the mail protocol that allows your account to sync with your phone. You can also enable POP (Post Office Protocol) if you wish, but this isn't necessary for Android access.

Labs, Themes, and Offline

These are settings that only apply to the web-based version of Gmail. Gmail Labs allows you to add experimental features that may or may not make it into the main release. Themes allow you to customize the look and feel of your Gmail web experience, and offline access lets you read and compose Gmail messages while not connected to the Internet. Messages sync once your Internet connection is resumed. Feel free to experiment and explore, but be aware that these settings do not transfer to your phone.

NOTE: One interesting Labs tool is Green Robot. This add-on turns the icons of chat buddies into robots if they're currently using Android for their chat session. It only works for Android, so you can't tell if they're chatting from an iPhone or BlackBerry. As with other Gmail Labs add-ons, this doesn't change anything in your Gmail phone app.

Understanding Gmail Mobile

There are two basic ways to access Gmail from your phone. Either you can use the Gmail app, or you can use the phone's web browser to access Gmail from the Web. When you use your web browser, by default you'll see a mobile version of Gmail that is trimmed down and simpler to use on phones.

The Gmail app on Android uses *push e-mail*. That means that you don't need to keep checking a web site. Your e-mail is always on and ready to receive new messages. This is just like keeping your desktop e-mail client on in the background when you use your laptop. It's the big advantage of the Android Gmail app over your phone's web browser, though the browser does have a few features missing in the Gmail app.

When new messages arrive, by default you'll see a notice in the status bar. You can drag down the status bar and click the notification to launch the Gmail app.

This chapter has covered quite a few web-based features, but there was an important reason to get to know them first. Most of these features cannot be changed from the Gmail app in Android, nor can they be changed from the mobile version of Gmail on the Web.

Web Version from Your Phone

If you are in a pinch and need to set up a filter or create a label, you can still do this from your phone. It just involves a bit of wrangling. Point your phone browser to http://mail.google.com. When you are logged in, scroll to the very bottom of the screen, and you'll see that you're viewing Gmail in mobile. Click the link next to that that says Desktop. What you see should be similar to Figure 6–3. The text is tiny, so you'll need to magnify your view and scroll around to navigate. You will still have fewer options than you would on your laptop's web browser. However, you still have all the options you need for effective phone use.

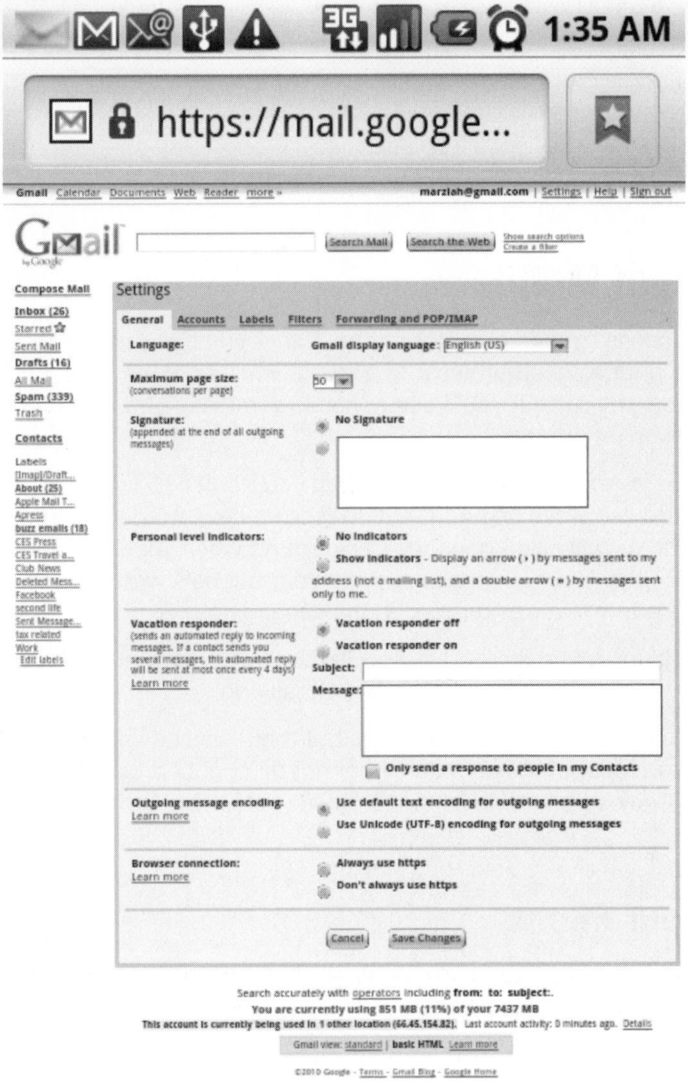

Figure 6–3. *Changing Gmail settings*

Sending and Replying to E-mail

Let's return to the Android Gmail app. If you want to send a message from within the Android app, navigate to the correct account, click the Menu button, and select Compose. You'll see something similar to Figure 6–4. If you're using a phone with a keyboard, you can slide it out or use the virtual keyboard.

Figure 6–4. *Composing e-mail*

Start typing in the To field, and Google will attempt to autocomplete the e-mail address from your contact list. If this is to a new contact, you'll just have to type the whole thing out. Use the trackball or your finger to navigate to the next fields.

If you want to add a picture attachment or more recipients, press the Menu button again. You'll have the option to add BCC and CC recipients and attachments from your phone's camera gallery. You can also choose to take a new picture to attach. Picture files are the only type of attachment supported on the default Android Gmail app, but you can still forward messages that contain other types of attachments.

When you're done with your message, press Send.

To reply to a message, open that message, scroll to the bottom of the message, and then press the Reply button. As with desktop e-mail programs, you can choose to reply or reply to all, and you can also choose to forward messages.

Android will automatically copy and append the entire message you're replying to. If you're used to paring down this message to highlight only the relevant section or insert something in the middle, you're out of luck. You can't edit the attached previous message, so just note the relevant parts in text.

Search

It's easy to get trapped into navigating through messages by the subject line and preview, but sometimes there's a faster way to find what you need. Google is known for search, so it's unsurprising to find a well-supported search tool within Gmail. Whenever you're in the Gmail app, press the Search button, and you can search through your messages. The search tool will autosuggest as you type.

Custom Signatures

If you set a signature on Gmail on the Web, that signature doesn't get included on e-mail you send from your phone. This gives you the chance to make a custom signature from your phone—perhaps something indicating that you're using a phone so that your recipient will be more willing to forgive short messages and the occasional typo.

To set your custom signature, press the Menu button from within the Gmail app while viewing the inbox of your account. Next, select Settings. You'll see the signature setting, and you can use this to create a text-only signature. When you're done press Save. That signature will only apply to messages sent from your phone for that specific account.

Notifications

While you're editing settings, it's a good time to think about notifications. Do you want a ringtone every time you get a message? Do you want the phone to vibrate? Do you want an update in your status bar? These are options listed under "Notification settings."

I get a lot of messages, so I silence the ringers and keep the option "Email notifications" checked so that I can glance and see if I have new messages. However, this is a setting that applies specifically to each e-mail account, so you could enable a ringtone for an urgent e-mail account and remove the notification for your personal e-mail.

Labels

Another way you can cut down on your inbox clutter is to only sync certain labels. Press Labels in the general settings of the account you want to change. You can choose how far back you want to sync messages in your inbox and which labels to sync on a case-by-case basis. I put an automatic filter on alerts from Facebook, for instance, and then I do not sync them from my phone.

Not syncing labels doesn't mean you can't still find the information, just like archiving a message doesn't mean it is inaccessible. Searching your inbox will still retrieve old messages. It just saves some phone memory and syncing time for things you don't need instantly available every time you launch the Gmail app.

Confirm Delete

If you check this item, you'll get an extra dialog every time you try to delete a message. If you're pretty sure with your fingers, leave it unchecked. I get nervous that I'll have a butterfinger moment and accidentally delete an important e-mail, so I leave this one checked.

Talk and Other Missing Gmail Features

Gmail on the Web has a chat window. This uses a variation of Google Talk, but it also allows for video and audio chats. Video chat isn't available for your phone, but with phones like the HTC EVO offering a video camera on the front of the phone, it's only a matter of time before it becomes available. Rather than accessing Chat through the Android Gmail app, you'll use the Google Talk app on your phone.

Task List

Another feature you may notice is a task list. It's a very handy to-do list tool. It's not included in the Gmail app; however, you can still use the task list. Simply navigate your web browser to http://gmail.com/tasks (or for Google Apps users, it will be http://mail.google.com/tasks/a/*your_domain*, with *your_domain* being the name of your domain). You can also make a shortcut for your Home screen. Create a bookmark of this address by pressing the star in your browser bar. Go to your Home screen and long-click. Select Shortcut ➤ Bookmark, and then find the task list.

Buzz

Google Buzz is a social networking component of Gmail. I'll talk about social networking tools in more detail later. Buzz isn't supported in the Gmail app on Android, but you can download a widget from Google that allows you to post updates, your location, and photos from your phone.

Multiple Google Accounts

If you're using Android 2.1 or above, you can set up multiple Gmail accounts on your Android phone. If you're using earlier versions, you can add multiple POP e-mail accounts to your Gmail account, but you can't have more than one Gmail inbox. The big difference is that, by setting up multiple Google accounts, you can set different ringtones for each Gmail account (or make all but one silent), and you don't share a single inbox.

Figure 6–5 shows multiple Gmail accounts. Unread messages are shown to the right of each account. If you click an account, you'll see only the inbox of that account. You can always get back to the view shown in Figure 6–5 by clicking the Menu button and selecting Accounts.

Figure 6–5. *Multiple accounts*

To add another Gmail account to your Android 2.1 or above phone, go to the Home screen and press the Menu button. Choose Settings ➤ "Accounts & sync." Next, press the button on the bottom of the screen labeled "Add account." Depending on the software installed on your phone, you'll generally have three choices: Google, Facebook, and Microsoft ActiveSync. If you've installed apps to connect with other accounts, you'll see more choices. For instance, my phone shows a choice for a TouchDown account, which is software for connecting to Exchange servers.

You can also add accounts from directly within the Gmail app by pressing the Menu button, going to Accounts, and then pressing the "Add account" button.

When you add another Google account, you'll be prompted to specify which parts of that account you want to sync. Your choices depend on what services you've used, but for e-mail accounts, you'll have the choice to sync Gmail and contacts.

Deleting Accounts

Deleting accounts is a reverse of the process for creating them. Just go to the Home screen and press the Menu button, and then go to Settings ➤ "Accounts & sync." Press the name of the account you want to delete, and press the "Remove account" button on the bottom of the screen. You'll get a warning message that you're about to delete an account, the e-mail, and the synced contacts, and you'll need to confirm to delete. Alternatively, you could just stop syncing an account if you wanted to retain your contacts.

The Email App

Android includes the Gmail app for adding Gmail accounts, but there's also an Email app for checking mail with non-Gmail accounts. Depending on your Exchange server's settings, this account can be used to check Exchange accounts as well as standard e-mail accounts that use POP or IMAP protocols.

The disadvantage of the Email app is that it uses pull e-mail for POP and IMAP accounts. Unlike push e-mail, where your e-mail account is always on and passively receives messages as they arrive, pull e-mail means that the Email app has to check the server every once in a while to see if you have new messages. You specify how often it does this in the settings. Check more often for quicker e-mail delivery, or check less often to save battery life.

Just like the Gmail app, you can add more than one account to the Email app in Android 2.1 and above. When you launch the Email app for the first time, it will prompt you to set up an e-mail account. On standard Android 2.1 and 2.2 phones, your choices for accounts are POP3, IMAP, and Microsoft Exchange ActiveSync, as shown in Figure 6–6. Your phone may have slightly different options if it uses an Android variation like HTC Sense or Motorola Blur.

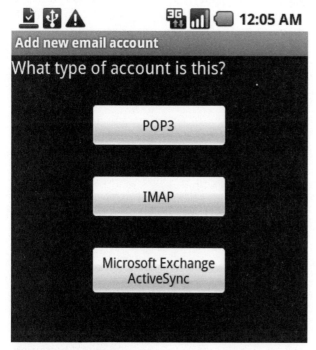

Figure 6–6. *Adding accounts*

Once you've added an account, you can keep adding more accounts from within the Email app by pressing the Menu button and then selecting Accounts ➤ "Add account." Just like with the Gmail app, you can customize notification settings by pressing the

Menu button and selecting "Account settings" from the account you want to modify. This is also where you set how frequently your phone checks for new e-mail.

Composing and replying to messages and adding attachments work the same way in the Email app as they do in the Gmail app. You can also flag messages with stars for later reference. You can't automatically filter messages, add labels, or put messages into folders.

Reading Attachments

Your ability to read attachments is going to depend on the type of attachment, the app you're using, and the software you have installed on your phone. If an e-mail has embedded pictures, just as with many desktop e-mail programs, you'll generally see a button to let you view the pictures.

Most Android e-mail apps support viewing some attachments, like Office 2003 documents, PDFs, images, and plain text documents, but not necessarily editing or saving them. If you receive an e-mail with an attachment, you can click the Open or Preview button to view it. If your device has more than one app capable of handling that file type, you'll see a dialog box like in Figure 6–7 that lets you choose how you want to handle the file. Click your preferred app, and you can view your attachment.

Figure 6–7. *Attachments*

Exchange Accounts on Android

By default, Android 2.1 and below does not fully support Exchange e-mail, and you're at the mercy of your IT department as to whether you can check it with the Email app. Your IT department might want to enforce security policy using Microsoft standards that just aren't supported in standard Android 2.1 and below installations. These policies might require certain lengths or types of passwords, data wiping for lost phones or failed passwords, timeouts after inactivity, or other options. You may very well have enabled those features, but your phone has to communicate back to the server that you're in compliance using Microsoft's protocols.

The default Email app in Android 2.1 and below doesn't support policy enforcement, so you will not be able to sync a G1 with your Exchange e-mail right out of the box if your business enforces security rules. Even if your IT department doesn't use policy enforcement and you have no problems syncing with your Exchange account, you won't get the full experience. You'll still be missing the Global Address List, and you won't be able to sync task and event requests through e-mail.

Many Android variations, like HTC Sense and MOTOBLUR, support push e-mail notification from Exchange ActiveSync, at least some security policy enforcement, and syncing of tasks and events. You're much more likely to be able to connect your Exchange account with these phones. Android 2.2 introduced support for security policy enforcement, remote data wiping, and auto-discovery (a server setting that makes setting up Exchange accounts much easier on your end). This makes the phone much more compatible with Exchange servers right out of the box.

Outlook Web Access

If you can't add an Exchange account through the Email app, you might be able to use an Outlook Web Access (OWA) account instead. The clear disadvantage is that this is an even worse arrangement than a pull e-mail. You have to actively check for e-mail yourself instead of getting notification that you've got a new message. If you use OWA to access mail, just set up a bookmark on your Home screen for quick access.

Third-Party Apps

If your phone doesn't have sufficient Exchange support, you can add that support through third-party apps. One popular app is TouchDown by NitroDesk. You can get more information here: www.nitrodesk.com/dk_touchdownFeatures.aspx.

TouchDown comes in both a free and paid version. The free version lets you check e-mail and get the day's calendar, while the $19.99 paid version, shown in Figure 6–8, allows you to sync your Exchange e-mail, accept and send task and event requests, use the Global Address List, and so on. TouchDown also supports security policy enforcement, so it should pass muster with most IT departments. You can also use it through OWA if you can't get it to work with ActiveSync. There's a fully functional free trial, so you can test to make sure everything works before you purchase it.

Figure 6–8. *TouchDown*

TouchDown is a really solid app. Not only does it provide most of the features of Outlook in your pocket, it also includes several widget options to keep your Exchange info handy whenever you use your phone. However, it doesn't mesh your e-mail, calendar, and task information with your other Android calendar, contacts, or task lists. On one hand it's handy to have business separate from personal life, and on the other hand it would be nice to have access to your Global Address List when using your main contact list.

Lotus Notes

IBM released an Android version of Lotus Notes, called Lotus Notes Traveler Companion, in June of 2010. It requires a phone running Android 2.0 or higher. There are also third-party apps available for Lotus Notes, such as MyLink Access for Lotus Notes, but these require you to install desktop software in order to work.

Summary

Android provides extensive support for the features of Gmail. If you happen to work for a company that has "gone Google" and uses Google Apps, you'll have an easy time configuring your phone to get to work quickly and easily. Take advantage of Gmail features like labels and automatic filters to keep your inbox organized.

For those using other e-mail systems, there's slightly more work involved. Using the Email app is still very similar to using the Gmail app, although it pulls e-mail instead of receiving push notifications.

There are several phone makers that have chosen to include Microsoft Exchange support, and there are quality third-party apps that support Exchange, so you can keep connected with your office from the road without having to rely on Google Apps.

Chapter 7

The Calendar

In this chapter, I'll go over the calendar. On Android phones, Google Calendar is the primary calendar, so I'll cover managing and using Google Calendar in more depth. Google Calendar is a web-based calendar, which means your dates and events are available on any computer or device that can access the Internet. Google Calendar was also built around collaboration. You can choose to share calendars and view public events. You can restrict your sharing to colleagues or open it up to friends and family members, and any combination in between.

However, not everyone has the luxury of choosing their workplace calendaring system. I'll also discuss Microsoft Outlook's calendar and Android, and we'll look at ways to import and export calendar events.

Using the Web-Based Google Calendar

Google Calendar stores its data in the cloud, but you can use a variety of methods to view that data, including the Internet, phone apps, and third-party tools that hook into Google's data. We'll approach it from the Web first, since that's where it was born. Google Calendar allows for multiple levels of privacy and the exporting and importing of data from standard formats. You could be using Google Calendar through either your personal account or through a business Google Apps account.

If you install the web browser plug-in Google Gears, you can also use Google Calendar when your computer is offline. The calendars will sync once you resume connection. Of course, your phone is meant to wander in and out of connection range, so there's nothing extra to install when using the phone version.

Figure 7–1 shows the basic web interface for Google Calendar. The middle area is the main calendar. On the right you'll see a task list. On the left are tools for creating and filtering calendars and events.

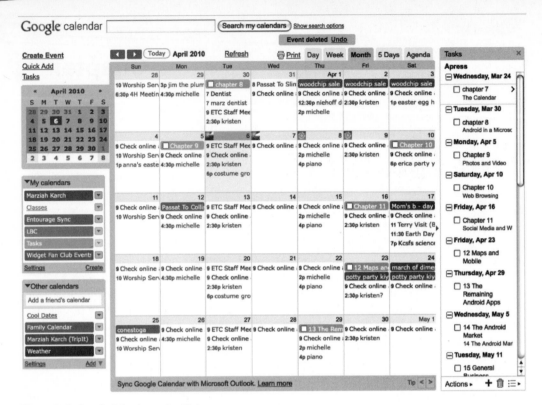

Figure 7–1. *Google Calendar on the Web*

Views

Google Calendar, like most calendar tools, has four basic views: month, week, day, and agenda. The agenda view shows all events in a chronological list. The web-based version of Google Calendar also has a print view that allows you to print whichever view you're using. Use this in case you'd like a dead-tree version of the calendar. Sometimes I'll print a backup copy of my schedule before business conventions, in case my phone and laptop batteries get drained.

NOTE: If you prefer, you can have Google e-mail a daily agenda. Click "Manage calendars" at the bottom left of the web page, and then click Notifications. There's a box labeled "Choose how you would like to be notified." If you check "Daily agenda," you'll receive a daily e-mail with agenda items from that calendar. Be sure to click the "Save" button.

Multiple Calendars

Rather than having one single calendar, Google Calendar operates as a series of calendars stacked on top of each other. Each calendar can be color coded and have different privileges in terms of privacy and sharing, so you can have a family calendar shared with your spouse and a work calendar shared by colleagues. You can also import public calendars with information like weather reports or holiday schedules.

You can share three basic permissions with calendars. You can share the ability to see busy blocks in the schedule, the ability to see event details, and the ability to edit calendars. Every calendar you can edit is listed under My Calendar. Every calendar you can only view is listed under Other Calendars.

In the web-based version of Google Calendar, these calendars will be on the left side of the screen, as shown in Figure 7–1.

You can control which calendars you see and how they're displayed by clicking the triangle next to the calendar's name (Figure 7–2). This is also one of many ways you can add events in your calendar.

Figure 7–2. *Controlling calendar settings*

> **NOTE:** Calendar Labs: Google likes to experiment with new features by putting them out as optional "Labs" add-ons. You can find some nice features, and if they're popular and work well, Google will roll them out into the main service. Generally speaking, these Labs experiments won't transfer to your phone, so don't be disappointed when they only work on the Web.

Adding Calendars

To add another calendar on the Web, click the Add link at the bottom of the "My calendars" area on the left. This is shown in Figure 7–3.

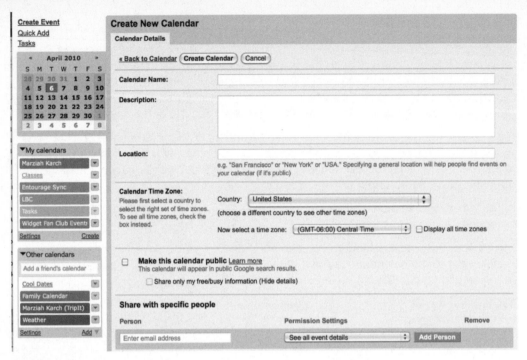

Figure 7–3. *Creating a new calendar*

You're given options to name and describe your new calendar. You can also optionally give a location, though this isn't necessary for private calendars. Specify your time zone if it's different from your default setting.

You can add a public calendar by its URL if you know it. Just add the URL in the "Other calendars" area.

Sharing Your Calendar

Now you need to choose sharing options. Your first choice is a private vs. a public calendar. Public calendars are visible to everyone. They can be useful for information like holidays, business hours, promotions, and sales, but not so useful for giving out your personal schedule to a few select friends, since everyone can see public events.

The next option is to share your calendar with specific people. If you don't plan on sharing the information with anyone, you can skip this step. If you want to share information with friends, coworkers, family members, or clients, you can enter their e-mail addresses here. You have to enter the addresses individually, but Google will autocomplete them as you type for anyone on your contact list.

If your business uses Google Apps, you will have an additional sharing option. Just below the option to make a calendar public, there will be an option to share your calendar with everyone on your web site domain.

Your sharing choices are:

- See only free/busy
- See all event details
- Make changes to events
- Make changes AND manage sharing

Anyone with "Make changes to events" access will be able to add events to your calendar, as well as edit events you've added. If you choose "Make changes AND manage sharing," the person you share this calendar with will be able to add other people to the calendar. This might be a good choice for sharing calendars with teams that might pull in other members during a project.

To change and view the settings on your calendars all at once, go to Settings ➤ "Calendar settings" and click the Calendars tab. From here you can change sharing privileges, unsubscribe (remove yourself from sharing), and delete calendars.

Deleting Calendars

You can always hide calendars rather than deleting them. If you're sure you'll never need a calendar again, click the Settings link below the "My calendars" list. You'll see a list of calendars. If you didn't create the calendar, you can't delete it; you can only unsubscribe from it. You can either unsubscribe from or delete calendars by clicking the appropriate link.

Google Apps Team Edition

If your workplace doesn't have Google Apps, there's a sneaky workaround. Google has a service called Google Apps Team Edition. If you register for Team Edition with your work e-mail, it creates a limited version of the Google Apps service for anyone with the same e-mail domain. You don't get a separate Gmail address, but you can take advantage of some of the Google Apps collaboration features, such as the ability to share documents or calendars with other members of your work team. You can register for an account at www.google.com/a.

Google also gave administrators the ability to turn off Google Apps Team Edition at any point in time, so be sure to share full permissions (choose "Make changes AND manage sharing") with your personal Gmail account, so you have a backup available if the calendar is erased.

Adding Events

On the Web, you can add events in one of many ways. Quick events can be added by clicking the "Quick add" link and then typing a short description of the event (e.g., "Pick up laundry at seven today" or "Dentist office at 3:00 on April 18" work fine). Click the Add button, and your event will be added to your default calendar.

You can also click any day or time slot, depending on your view, to quickly add an event. In this case, it will already know the date. Just type in a quick description and select the proper calendar from the drop-down menu. You can also add to-do items as a task by clicking a day and then clicking the task link.

You can go into more detail by clicking "Create event" on the left side of the screen. This will bring up a detailed list of options, including what, where, when, whether the event repeats, whether your time should be listed as busy or available, and who should be invited to attend.

If you elect to override the privacy options, you should know that making an event private means it's only visible to people with editing privileges, not that it's only visible to you. Making an event public means you share event details with anyone who would otherwise only see the time as busy. It won't make an event visible in search.

Adding Guests

Use the detailed "Create event" link or click the "Edit details" link in other views to invite others to your event. You'll see the "Add guests" box. Here you can add e-mail addresses, select options, and press the + Add guests button to add guests to your invite list. Depending on which options you select, guests can invite others, modify the event, or see who else was invited. This only applies to the event, not your entire calendar. All your invited attendees will receive an e-mail.

If your recipient doesn't have Google Calendar, they can still accept or decline your invitation. Google Calendar events are sent in iCalendar (iCal) format, which is an industry standard that can be imported into nearly every calendar program, including Microsoft Outlook.

Importing and Exporting Calendars

If you want to get calendar events into or out of Google Calendar, click the Settings link in the upper-right corner or use the link just under the "My calendars" list. You'll see a link in the Calendars tab for importing and exporting calendars. Google uses iCal format to export, and it can import iCal or CSV, which is Microsoft Outlook format.

Syncing Calendars with Exchange

If you're using a Microsoft Exchange server to manage your company events, you may want to sync it with Google Calendar to make work and home life easier. You can sync your calendars by downloading and installing Google Calendar Sync from Google at http://dl.google.com/googlecalendarsync/GoogleCalendarSync_Installer.exe.

When you install Google Calendar Sync, you can decide if this is a two-way sync, where events are editable in both programs, or a one-way sync, where events are only editable in one program. If you're using another calendar, such as TouchDown, you may want to just sync in one direction to avoid having everything show up twice.

If you're a Mac user, syncing between Google Calendar and Exchange is trickier. Users of OS X 10.5 and above can sync between Apple's calendar program, iCal, and Google Calendar using the CalDAV protocol. However, that may not actually sync Exchange events, since those are syncing on a separate calendar. You can duplicate entries or use a third-party tool on your Mac, but it may be more cost effective to just buy an Exchange-syncing app for your phone.

Exchange Syncing on Android 2.2

Android 2.2, Froyo, has better Exchange syncing than previous versions of Android, and allows calendar events to sync along with e-mail. If you're using Android 2.2 and using the Mail app on your phone to retrieve your work e-mail, you don't need to install any desktop-syncing software. Your work-related calendar entries will show up on your calendar on your phone only, not on the Web.

Using Google Calendar on Android

Now that we've gone over the web version of Google Calendar, let's discuss how it works on your phone. The Android version of Google Calendar comes preinstalled on most Android phones. In versions 2.1 and 2.2, it even comes with a widget to display one day at a time. HTC Sense phones have a very slick widget that looks different from the standard Android, but this only changes the appearance; the data still comes from Google Calendar.

Like Gmail, you can either use the native Calendar app, or you can access Google Calendar from your mobile web browser by going to `m.google.com/calendar`, as shown in Figure 7–4. The mobile version of Google Calendar is rather limited. Your view is restricted to either day or month, and your only settings choices are which calendars to display. You can, however, easily navigate to the mobile Tasks list or other mobile versions of tools. In a pinch, you can also force Google Calendar to display the nonmobile version by clicking the Desktop link at the bottom of the page.

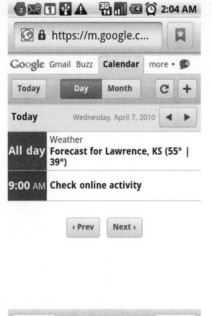

Figure 7–4. *Mobile version of Google Calendar*

Tasks

If you have to-do items you need to complete, you might want to see the deadlines in your calendar. You can do this in the web-based version of Google Calendar, but the Android version of Google Calendar doesn't display your tasks. That doesn't mean you can't use the tool, however. To add your own Google tasks, use the instructions from Chapter 6 and create a bookmark to the mobile Google Tasks web site, at https://mail.google.com/tasks, or use the third-party app gTasks, which syncs with Google Tasks.

You can also skip Google Tasks entirely and use a third-party app like TouchDown, Remember the Milk, or Astrid for managing your to-do lists.

Google Calendar on Android 2.1 and above comes with a widget for easily seeing your daily schedule, as shown in Figure 7–5. You can long-click the Home screen to add this widget if it's not there already. HTC Sense phones come with a larger, slicker widget that also gives you a month or transparent agenda view. You can download Pure Grid or Pure View through the Android Market if you want to simulate the Sense experience.

Figure 7–5. *Calendar widget*

You can launch the Calendar app by clicking the widget or the Calendar icon. When you launch the Calendar app, you'll notice it's much more user-friendly than the mobile web app. You can view events by day, week, month, today, and agenda. Today is just a handy shortcut to view the current date on whatever view you're using.

Press your phone's Menu button to switch to a different view, as shown in Figure 7–6. The choice you aren't offered is your current view. Navigate between months, weeks, and days by swiping your finger side to side on day and week views, and up and down on month views.

Just as with the desktop web version, your view dictates how much of an event preview you can see. On the month view, the screen real estate is small enough that you won't see any text. You'll see graphic bars to indicate relatively how busy a day is and when during the day events will occur. You can click a day to switch to the day or agenda view (depending on the last one you used) and see more details. In the week view, you can see a few characters of your event title. Click an event to view the event details. The day view shows event titles, and the agenda view shows event titles and summaries.

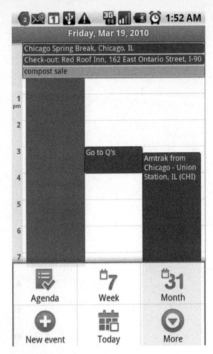

Figure 7–6. *Views*

Adding Events

When you need to add an event, press your phone's Menu button, and then click the "New event" button, as shown in Figure 7–6. You'll see the "Event details" screen, as shown in Figure 7–7. You can use your phone's scroll bar to navigate down the list and add all the relevant details. You can also create an all-day event, set an event to repeat, invite guests, and set reminders. Click Done to save your changes.

Keep in mind that this syncs with the Web, so you can also make a short entry on your phone and add more detail when you have access to a larger keyboard.

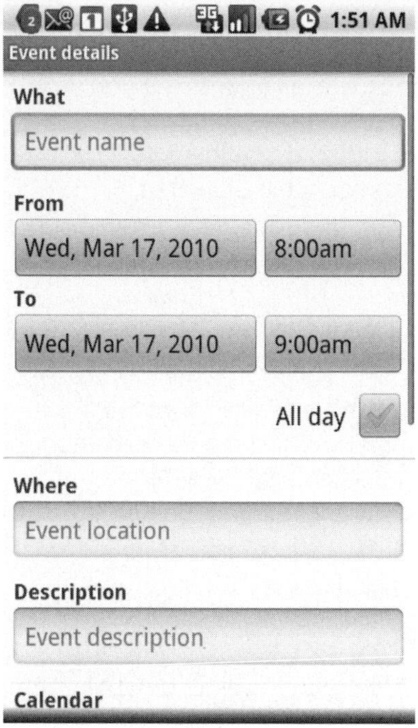

Figure 7–7. *Event details*

Deleting and Editing Events

To delete or edit an event, go to the "View event" screen. You get there by clicking an event in day, week, or agenda view. You'll have to click twice from month view, since the first click will get you to the day or agenda view. Once you see the "View event" screen, press the Menu button. You can also just long-click an event in any view and select "View event."

You should see the options to edit or delete the item. If you don't see this choice, and you're viewing the correct screen, one of two things is going on. You cannot delete events you did not create, and you cannot edit events on calendars where you don't have editing privileges.

If you're in day or week view, long-clicking an event should also bring up choices to edit or delete an item.

There's no option to drag and drop events to new time slots like you see on some desktop calendar programs, so if you need to move an event to a new time, you'll need to edit the event details. This is probably a wise move, since dragging and dropping items on a screen you have to touch all the time might lead to a lot of inadvertently shifted appointments.

Inviting Attendees and Accepting Invitations

The event details allow you to invite attendees to events by e-mail address. If you've invited others or have been invited to an event, you'll see additional information in the event view. If you've been invited, you'll have a button to indicate whether you'll be attending the event. Everyone invited to the event will also see a list of invited participants and their attendance status. If you like, you can go into your Calendar app's settings (Menu ➤ More ➤ Settings) and check the box to hide events you've declined.

Managing Your Calendars

Google Calendar likes to use multiple calendars, but you can't add new ones from the Android app. You can turn existing calendars off and on by pressing the Menu button, and then clicking "more" ➤ "My calendars." Note that this has a slightly different meaning from "My calendars" in Android. It refers to every calendar you have permission to see, not just the ones you can edit.

Setting Alerts, Alarms, and Reminders

It's great to have a calendar, but sometimes you need some reminders. In order to add them, got to Menu ➤ More ➤ Settings. You can use the options here to set your default alert settings, including ringtones, alert windows that pop up, and vibration. You can also set the default amount of time to be reminded before an event occurs.

I prefer my phone not to ring when I'm already on my way to a meeting, so I set the ringtone to silent. I also check the vibrate option and set my "Alerts & notifications" setting to give me a status bar notification.

You can add a reminder to or remove it from any event by going to the event view and clicking the green + labeled "Add reminder." You can also override the default time (e.g., so you don't get reminded about your flight 10 minutes before it leaves). You can even add more than one reminder to the same event. You might use this to add a reminder the day before your flight and another one just before you need to drive to the airport the day of your flight.

Additional Phone Options

Do you want to get SMS reminders for events? You can set this up in the Calendar Settings in the desktop web version of Google Calendar. Go to Settings ➤ Mobile Setup, as shown in Figure 7–8. Fill out your phone number, and verify it by typing in the text message Google texts you. Once you verify your phone number, you'll receive text reminders. Keep in mind that this could cost you money if you don't have unlimited text messaging.

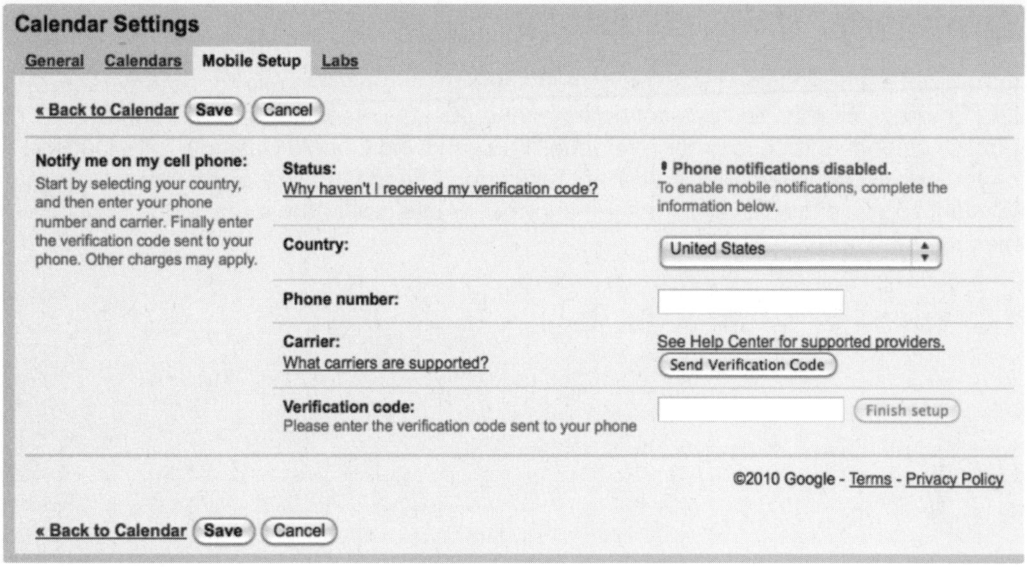

Calendar Settings

General   Calendars   **Mobile Setup**   Labs

« Back to Calendar (Save) (Cancel)

Notify me on my cell phone:
Start by selecting your country, and then enter your phone number and carrier. Finally enter the verification code sent to your phone. Other charges may apply.

Status:
Why haven't I received my verification code?

! Phone notifications disabled.
To enable mobile notifications, complete the information below.

Country: United States

Phone number:

Carrier: See Help Center for supported providers.
What carriers are supported?   (Send Verification Code)

Verification code: (Finish setup)
Please enter the verification code sent to your phone

©2010 Google - Terms - Privacy Policy

« Back to Calendar (Save) (Cancel)

Figure 7–8. *Mobile setup*

Using Other Calendar Apps

Google Calendar is the primary calendar for Android, but that doesn't mean you're stuck with it. Rather than syncing your events with Google Calendar Sync, you can keep them within a separate calendar. Nitro Desk TouchDown is a $24 app that syncs with your Outlook calendar and has a separate calendar widget.

Leaky Nozzle Firehouse Scheduler is a $5.99 app that offers a calendar geared toward scheduling shifts in a fire department. It also tracks vacation time. The myDAY journal app is $1.49 and allows you to keep a simple journal in chronological order and export the data or view it on a calendar. The fonts are a bit much, but it is very useful for keeping records of the time you've spent on projects during the day.

Need to use a calendar other than the Gregorian? Alternative Calendar has both free and paid features, but the free version allows you to view a variety of other calendars, such as Islamic, Chinese, Bahai, Hebrew, and Ethiopian. You can also overlay it with a Gregorian calendar, so you have a point of reference. This calendar doesn't let you save events, but it does let you check to make sure you aren't calling a business contact on a religious holiday.

There are also tons of apps that enhance the default Android calendar tools. IRT Calendar is a $5.99 app that provides enhancements to Google Calendar, such as more views and icons for easier navigation in the agenda view. Smooth Calendar is a free widget for a better agenda view. Hawkmoon Software offers $1.99 productivity enhancements to the calendar for calculating the number of workdays for projects or trial dates.

Summary

In Android, Google Calendar is the default calendar. It's easy to use for both personal and business events. You can set up team and private calendars, and you can even publish calendars for customer reference. You can sync Google Calendar with Outlook or you can use an alternative calendar. Tasks don't tie to Google Calendar's mobile version, so you either have to create a shortcut or use one of the many third-party task management apps.

Chapter 8

Android in a Microsoft World

Business lives in a Microsoft world, so if you want your phone to work for you, you'll need to figure out ways to get your phone to work with Microsoft. The Android OS is based on Linux, but that doesn't mean it's totally shut off from Microsoft. Microsoft has belatedly embraced cloud computing and cross-platform compatibility in recent years. Microsoft even released a bar code scanning app for Android in March 2010: Tag Reader. As I'm writing this, there are also rumors that Microsoft will develop an Android version of Silverlight. Silverlight is a competitor to Flash, and Microsoft has always intended it to run on multiple platforms.

That doesn't mean you'll ever have seamless support for Microsoft when using any platform other than Microsoft's. For example, the Mac version of Word doesn't support the same features as the Windows version. If you use a lot of advanced features, you're going to find bugs and files that just won't display correctly. That said, you *can* use Android in a Microsoft world and still get your work done.

In this chapter, I'll review some ways to connect your phone to Microsoft Exchange servers, I'll talk about SharePoint and other Microsoft technologies, including Office 2010 and Office 2010 web apps. I'll also discuss some alternatives to Microsoft you can use in a pinch.

Using Android with Exchange Servers

As discussed in Chapter 6, Android 2.1 and below has some support for Exchange e-mail, but it doesn't support many of the security policies many IT departments require. In some cases, you may be forced to use Outlook Web Access (OWA). In addition, Android doesn't sync your Outlook calendar, Global Address List, or Outlook task requests. Android 2.2 offers better support for Exchange, including security policies, remote wiping, and the Global Address Book. It also allows Exchange calendar syncing. It still does not share tasks, though.

Motorola phones with MOTOBLUR may have better support for Exchange and security policies. That doesn't mean you're out of luck if you have a different phone, however. There are a number of third-party tools that offer corporate Exchange compatibility for under $30. Among the solutions are DataViz RoadSync, Moxier Mail, and NitroDesk TouchDown. Of those solutions, TouchDown is probably the best bet, since it offers a free, fully functional trial. That way you can make absolutely sure it is compatible with your phone and your Exchange server's security policies.

Exchange compatibility is something that is likely to improve over time. Customers demand the ability to check their corporate e-mail accounts, and Google, phone manufacturers, and app developers have all been listening. Android's next release, Gingerbread, will likely improve corporate compatibility even further.

Exchange Calendar Options

As discussed in Chapter 7, you can either use a third-party tool like TouchDown to bypass Google Calendar or you can use tools like Google Calendar Sync to duplicate entries between your Exchange and Google calendars. Android 2.2 Exchange support includes calendar syncing. What you do depends on your personal style and whether or not you're authorized to install software on a computer that syncs with Exchange.

Using Android with SharePoint Servers

If your company uses a SharePoint server for collaborative document sharing, you may or may not be able to directly access the server from your phone. According to Microsoft documentation, SharePoint doesn't specifically support Android's web browser.

Depending on your configuration, you might be able to log in, and you might be able to download files for later viewing. You've got a better chance with version 2007 and above. I've had mixed results when trying to use SharePoint 2007 from Android, and those results probably largely depended on the settings. On one server I was able to log in and access files, and on another I wasn't even permitted to enter my username and password. If you're able to access files, you'll generally have "level 2" browser support, meaning that you won't be able to view documents inline, sync to Outlook, or edit documents at the click of a button.

When SharePoint was originally designed, Microsoft envisioned a corporate intranet where devices and software were strictly controlled, so it initially only supported Internet Explorer, and grudgingly added browser support as SharePoint started being used for public-facing pages instead of just intranets.

In SharePoint 2010, Microsoft has not listed specific support for Android's web browser, but that also doesn't rule it out. Cross-platform compatibility was one of the selling points Microsoft used to pitch SharePoint 2010 at Web 2.0 Expo. In my testing, SharePoint 2010 allows Android's web browser to download and upload files.

That said, there are features that will always be unavailable from Android's web browser, including any SharePoint features that depend on ActiveX controls. ActiveX is a desktop Windows-specific technology. It doesn't even run on Windows Mobile. It's also unlikely that Microsoft will release Android versions of Office, and it's therefore unlikely you'll be able to have seamless offline editing in SharePoint like you can on your PC. Microsoft is building enhanced compatibility with SharePoint into Windows Phone 7 as a selling point.

If you need access to SharePoint and cannot get there from your phone, you could either tether your phone to a laptop (I'll discuss this in a later chapter) or use a VNC connection to remotely view the files from your desktop computer.

Using Android with Windows SkyDrive

One product of Microsoft's embrace of cloud computing is SkyDrive. Part of Windows Live, SkyDrive allows you to upload files from your computer and share them with just about any other device. If you want to share files with your phone, SkyDrive works like a charm. However, it is not a two-way street. You can't upload files from Android to SkyDrive yet.

To get started with SkyDrive, go to http://skydrive.live.com from your desktop computer. Once you've registered for an account, you can access SkyDrive from Android using the same address in your phone's browser.

To get around SkyDrive's upload limitations, you can use SMEStorage at www.smestorage.com through the web browser on your phone. You can also use SkyDrive Simple Viewer on your Windows desktop to find the WebDAV addresses for your SkyDrive folders. You'll then need to download a WebDAV app for Android, such as DavDrive or Mobile Webdav.

Other Windows Live services, like Photos, Hotmail, MSN Messenger, and Spaces, can be accessed from your phone's mobile browser, too. Go to http://mobile.live.com, as shown in Figure 8–1.

Figure 8–1. *Windows Live Mobile*

Third-Party Solutions for Handling Office Documents

Knowing you can download documents is cold comfort if you can't do anything with them. Fortunately, you can view and even edit Microsoft Office documents with the help of some third-party tools. The most important thing to ask yourself as you evaluate apps is just how much you need them to do. Do you just need to view Office files, or do you need the ability to edit them? The following subsections describe a variety of apps you can choose from depending on your needs.

QuickOffice

QuickOffice is an easy app for viewing Office Word and Excel files. It ships with the HTC DROID ERIS; the Motorola CLIQ, DEXT, and DROID; and the Google Nexus One. That means if you own one of those phones, you'll be able to view attachments without having to worry about downloading a new tool.

However, QuickOffice is a view-only tool, and it won't save or copy attachments to your *Secure Digital* or SD card. It can be purchased for $13 on phones that don't ship with it pre-installed, but that isn't a competitive price for the feature set.

DataViz Documents To Go

If your phone didn't come with QuickOffice, you can also download the free version of DataViz Documents To Go. If you need the ability to actually edit files, the paid version of Documents To Go is under $15 and allows viewing, creating, and editing for PowerPoint, Excel, and Word files. You can also use it for view-only access to Adobe PDF files.

You won't be able to edit every file in exactly the same way as you would from a desktop computer. You can't insert pictures into PowerPoint slides or fine-tune the formatting on a Word file. That's just unworkable, and it's doubtful you'd really want to write an entire proposal with a thumb keyboard. However, you can fix that quick typo in a presentation on the road, as shown in Figure 8–2.

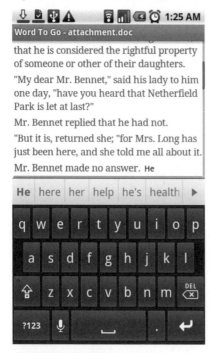

Figure 8–2. *Word To Go*

Once you've edited a document you receive as an e-mail attachment, be sure to save the changes by pressing the Menu button and clicking File ➤ Save. You can also elect to send files as e-mail attachments using this method.

ThinkFree Mobile Office

ThinkFree Office is a low-cost, Microsoft Office-compatible word processing suite that runs on Java. The Android version allows you to view and browse Office files (editing capability is planned for future releases). ThinkFree Mobile Office for Android comes preinstalled on Samsung Galaxy phones, and for other phones it can be purchased for $10. You can also purchase individual components for $5, including ThinkFree Write, ThinkFree Calc, and ThinkFree Present.

The largest advantage of ThinkFree Office is that it comes with a built-in file browser, which makes it easier to retrieve files from your phone's SD card, as shown in Figure 8–3. If you're an existing ThinkFree Online user, you can also conveniently upload and download files between your phone and the ThinkFree web space. Just long-click a file from within the ThinkFree browser and choose the appropriate option.

Figure 8–3. *ThinkFree Mobile*

Managing Downloads

Just where do all those downloaded files go, anyway? When you view an e-mail attachment, it most likely will not be downloaded anywhere, but if you view documents from other web services, such as SharePoint 2007, they're often downloaded to your SD card. Android doesn't make it easy to browse through your downloaded files, so the best solution is to find an app that adds that ability. ThinkFree Mobile comes with a visual file browser. Documents To Go allows you to open files from your SD card, but the navigation is somewhat clumsy.

ES File Explorer is a free app that allows you to visually explore the contents of your SD card, as shown in Figure 8–4. Files that you download from web sites like SharePoint 2007 will usually end up in a folder called "download," while files that you create or save from e-mail attachments will usually end up in a "documents" folder.

Figure 8–4. *ES File Explorer*

You can move files from one folder to another, but not through drag-and-drop. Long-click the file you wish to move, select Cut, and then navigate to the destination folder. Press the Menu button, select Operations, and then select Paste.

Emailing Files

Now that you've downloaded files and found where they're stored, how do you move them somewhere else? You may have noticed when trying to attach a file to an e-mail message that Android only allows you to attach pictures this way. Not to worry—you can use ES File Explorer to navigate to the file you want to send. Long-click the file, select Send, and then choose an e-mail app. Using this method, you can even choose to send your e-mail through TouchDown. Once you've made your selection, you'll start a new e-mail message with your attachment already included. Just fill in the To, From, Subject, and Content fields.

Microsoft Office and Web Apps

With Microsoft Office 2010, Microsoft introduced the idea of working with documents online. You can view and edit Office files from Microsoft Office Workspace using standard web browsers and Office desktop software. You can't edit files on Android, but you can still open them using Microsoft Office Workspace on the Web at http://workspace.officelive.com.

That means your colleagues can still share documents that you can preview on the road, and you can send them feedback. There are a few caveats. Office Live Workspace is still very new, and it doesn't officially support Android's web browser. The interface, as shown in Figure 8–5, is not mobile browser-friendly. You can navigate it, but it involves a lot of zooming in and out and panning around. Sharing and viewing documents works from Android, but downloading, editing, saving, and commenting do not work at this time.

Figure 8–5. *Office Live Workspace*

OneNote vs. Evernote

If you've been using Microsoft's OneNote for gathering clippings and notes and collaborative sharing, I've got bad news and good news. The bad news is that there isn't a solution for OneNote on Android. None of the Office-compatible apps I've reviewed has listed OneNote support, and OneNote 2010's mobile support is planned to be through Windows mobile devices.

The good news is that there's a less expensive alternative, Evernote. You can get started at www.evernote.com and download the free Evernote app (Figure 8–6) through the Android Market. Evernote allows you to create web clippings, make small notes, and view files through multiple platforms on multiple devices. You can also take audio notes from your phone and then transcribe them from your desktop.

Figure 8–6. *Evernote*

The free version allows you to save personal notes and a limited number of file types. The premium version for $45 per year allows you to share access to notes and upload unlimited file types. It also provides better encryption for sensitive corporate data.

Microsoft may relent and release an Android version of OneNote, and doesn't rule out third-party app support; however, for many users, Evernote already has Microsoft beat.

Google Docs

Google provides another solution for document collaboration, Google Docs. Google Docs is a free service that allows you to create and collaborate on word processing documents, spreadsheets, surveys, drawings, and presentations. Google Docs also lets you import and export Office-compatible files. However, you may lose formatting and options in some cases.

If you use Google Docs, you can still view your files from Android. You can edit spreadsheets, as shown in Figure 8–7, but you can only view other files at this time. It still comes in handy for reviewing slides right before giving a presentation. You can also use the third-party app GDocs for downloading and syncing Google Docs files with your Android device. Google has a vested interest in Android support, and there are a number of Android tablets due out before Christmas 2010, so expect improved Android compatibility in the future.

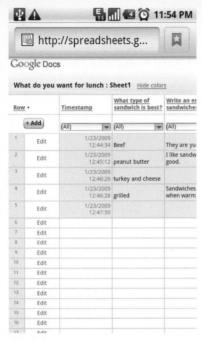

Figure 8–7. *Google Docs Spreadsheet*

Rather than rely on the check-in, check-out system used in SharePoint 2007 and earlier, Google Docs allows multiple users to view and edit files simultaneously. Users who are viewing the same file see a chat window to let them discuss the document while they edit. Spreadsheets also allow you to embed gadgets for enhanced tasks, such as pie charts, maps, and more. Chat windows and gadget support is asking a bit much for a lowly phone screen, and it's not supported at this time. As Android gains popularity in larger screens, this is also an area that will likely become more equivalent to desktop browsers.

To get started with Google Docs, use your Google account and log into http://docs.google.com.

Summary

Your individual phone may already have software preinstalled to allow it to more easily coexist with Microsoft. There is no perfect solution, but not even Microsoft's own mobile platform provides support for every Office desktop software feature.

If you select the right software tools and web apps, you can preview, download, and even edit Microsoft Office files. Files are generally saved on your SD card, so using a file-browsing app like ES File Explorer helps you better manage the content and send it as an e-mail attachment. Both Google and Microsoft have web-based solutions for viewing word processing documents online, and Evernote provides a fantastic alternative to OneNote. Most solutions only allow you to preview Office files, but Documents To Go also allows you to edit and save files.

Chapter 9

Photos and Video

Camera phones are not a new phenomenon, but only recently have those cameras improved to the point that you could leave your point-and-shoot behind and still end up with decent photos. Not every phone is created equal when it comes to cameras, so make sure you look at the camera when you shop for a phone.

Whether you need to document work sites or scan bar codes, this chapter will get you up and running with Android photography. I'll discuss a few digital camera basics, like megapixels and image size. I'll also talk about how to adjust your cameras for different lighting conditions, and how to turn the flash on and off (if you have one).

You'll also learn how to enhance your photos and share them by e-mail, Internet, and MMS (picture texting). Finally, you'll learn about using your phone to take video footage, and some of the apps that will make your photography and video session shine.

Understanding Your Camera

Before going into the nitty gritty of shooting photos, let's discuss the camera on your phone. Since there is no standard, one-size-fits-all Android phone, there's no standard Android camera—the HTC Evo even comes with two cameras, However, there are a few things most phone cameras have in common.

So far, none of them will match the quality you'd find in a DSLR (digital single-lens reflex) camera. This is the type of professional camera with a separate lens and body that lets you adjust just about everything and change lenses for specific purposes, such as long distances or wide angles. DSLRs are expensive, large, and heavy, and we don't have the technology to fit them in a phone . . . yet. Likewise, you won't find the video quality in a phone that you will in a dedicated digital video camera, and phones just don't have the memory to store large, uncompressed video files.

However, if your job does not require professional high-end photography or video, it is entirely possible to use your phone for these purposes, and avoid having to carry around two or three separate devices. There are a few things to keep in mind as you shop for a new phone with photography in mind.

Megapixels and Image Size

Each square on a monitor or phone display is a pixel. A megapixel is a million pixels, or 1000×1000 pixels. Webcams are generally either a low-quality .3 megapixels (close to the size of old standard-definition television broadcasts) or 1.3 megapixels, the size of an SXGA (1280×1024) monitor. Neither of those is large enough to yield satisfying print results, because of yet another dimension, pixels per inch (ppi) (also called dots per inch, or dpi).

When you display images on a monitor, 72 dpi looks fine. However, if you print that same image, it will look horrible at that resolution. You'll be able to see every pixel. If you're printing, you want an image somewhere around the 250 to 300 dpi range for good print results; most professionals use 300 dpi as the standard. That means, to get a quality 8×10-inch photo, you need a camera with at least 5 megapixels for a 250 dpi print and 7.2 megapixels for a 300 dpi print.

The first commercial Android phone, the T-Mobile G1, has a 3.2-megapixel camera. That's enough resolution to print a 300 dpi 5×7-inch photo, but no larger. There's no flash on the camera, so it doesn't handle low light well. The Nexus One and Motorola DROID cameras both ship with 5-megapixel cameras with flash. The Sony Ericsson Xperia X10 has an 8-megapixel camera, as does the HTC EVO. In fact, the EVO has an 8-megapixel camera on the back and a 1.3-megapixel camera on the front for video conferencing. Every phone I've tried has had a second or two lag in response when you press the button to snap a photo, but that's likely to improve as hardware improves.

Video resolution is lower than print resolution. High-definition (HD) video is at maximum just slightly bigger than 2 megapixels. However, video struggles against the amount of space it takes up, so most phones do not support HD video at this time.

Zoom and Focus

Point-and-shoot cameras come with either fixed focus or autofocus. Fixed-focus cameras are optimized to take a photo with the same focus—usually from a couple of feet to infinity. They use the same aperture opening and shutter speed for every single picture. That means anything too close will be out of focus. This is the type of focus you get with disposable cameras, because it's cheap and doesn't require any sort of adjustment on the user's end.

Autofocus cameras change the focus by using software and hardware adjustments. The biggest difference you'll notice as a user is that you can focus on things very near the camera lens, such as bar codes. It also means you'll have more out-of-focus pictures, since the autofocus might not always work quite as well as you'd hoped, but the overall picture quality will be better. Very few Android cameras come without autofocus. The HTC Tattoo is one of the few fixed-focus phones sold in the United States.

Zoom is another feature often listed on cameras. There are two types of zoom: optical and digital. Optical zooms use the camera's lens (the camera optics) to magnify part of the photo frame. You can still get a high-resolution photo from an optical zoom. Digital zoom is just a software solution in which the camera makes part of the picture look bigger. It's the illusion of zoom without adding any detail to the picture. When possible, it's best to ignore digital zoom and just stand closer to the subject of your photo or video. However, that's not always possible, and that's when digital zoom is useful.

Taking a Picture

A lot of this chapter is going to depend on which phone you use. Not only are there differences in physical hardware, but different versions of Android have different camera capabilities, and phone manufacturers are free to offer additional software. Android 1.5 offered very rudimentary camera functions and few options, but Android 2.2 offers more choices.

To take a picture, either press the physical camera button on your phone or launch the Camera app from the app tray or your Home screen. Other software may also allow you to use your phone's camera, some of which I'll discuss later. Figure 9–1 shows the Camera app on a Nexus One running Android 2.1.

Figure 9–1. *Taking a picture*

In this case, the phone is held on its side for a horizontally framed photo, but you can take photos vertically, too. Unlike with some apps, the position of the buttons on the screen will not change as you rotate the phone orientation.

On the right side of the screen, you'll see a small preview of the last photo you took, a slider to slide from video to still-photography mode, and a shutter button to take the photo. On the left, you'll see visual indications about your camera settings. In Figure 9–1, the photo is set to allow geotagging, and the flash is set to be automatically triggered in low lighting. In Android 2.2, these visual indications have been moved to the right and combined with the buttons that allow you to change settings.

To take a photo, simply click the shutter button at the bottom-right corner of the screen. You'll notice a second or two delay before the picture snaps. While this is often frustrating when trying to get the perfect picture, it also gives the camera a chance to refocus after you've pressed the button.

On the Nexus One, there's no way to adjust focus by pressing on the desired focal point, as there is on the iPhone. You can only choose between letting Android do the focusing with autofocus, and setting the camera to "infinity" mode. You can use digital zoom on phones that support it by pressing on the screen until the + and – buttons appear; or, in Android 2.2, by pressing the zoom slide adjuster at the lower-right corner of the screen, as shown in Figure 9–2.

Figure 9–2. *Zoom in Android 2.2*

Once you snap a photo in Android 2.1, it will appear as a preview on the corner of the screen. If you tap the preview, you'll see the full photo for review, as shown in Figure 9–3. If you tap the center of the screen, the + or – magnification buttons will appear. Press on the + side to zoom in, and drag the photo around with your finger to examine parts of it. The pinch-to-zoom action does not work in Android 2.1 and below, but it does work in Android 2.2. When you press on the review picture, you'll also see arrows on either side of the screen. Use these to browse through other pictures on your camera. In Android 2.2, you'll go directly to that picture in the Gallery app, which is one of the reasons pinch-to-zoom works.

Figure 9–3. *Reviewing photos*

Also notice the quick options on the left. You can delete a photo, share it, and set it as a contact or wallpaper; or click the Done button to exit review mode and get back to the main Camera app. You can also press the Menu button for more options, such as rotating and cropping the photo or viewing the metadata. Depending on the photo's settings, you may also see a Show on Maps option. I'll discuss some of these options in more detail later in this chapter.

Selecting the Optimal Settings

Android 1.6 and earlier allow you to change the size of your picture by pressing the Menu button when using the main Camera app. This could be useful if you want to take more pictures and are running out of storage space, or you want to send your photos by MMS.

In Android 2.1, you can press the Menu button and then select Settings, but the easier solution is to drag open the Camera app's advanced settings tray (which you can see on the left in Figure 9–1, shown previously). The advanced settings menu is shown in Figure 9–4.

In Android 2.2, this became even easier, and your settings are displayed as an onscreen overlay, as shown in Figure 9–2. Simply click the appropriate symbol and adjust the settings. Notice that the icon changes after you adjust an item to give you a visual clue about your settings.

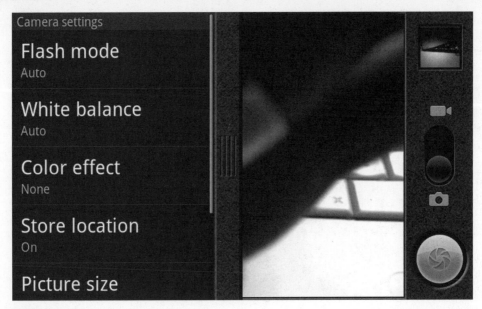

Figure 9–4. *Camera advanced settings menu*

Depending on your camera and your phone, you can turn your flash on or off. This is helpful if you want to take pictures in a museum where flash isn't allowed, or you want to take a picture of someone who is lit from behind and the camera sensors don't detect that you need the extra light.

White balance is a way to remove color imbalances in your pictures, so white shows up as white. You can leave this set to automatic, but if you notice that pictures look funny in incandescent lighting or seem to consistently have an odd color cast, try adjusting this setting.

Some phones let you play with digital color effects like sepia tones and simulated solarization. Remember that you can always alter a photo after you take it with the right software, but you can't change a photo with a color effect back to the original settings after you've snapped it.

The "Store location" setting allows you to specify whether your camera will include your geographic location in a photo's metadata. Use this to keep track of exactly where you took photos on vacations or during field work. This is why some photos offer a Show on Maps option when you review them. Keep in mind that others will also be able to see your geotagging data if you upload these types of photos to the Web.

Your picture size and quality settings depend heavily on your hardware. If you have no need for large photos, by all means keep the file size small and adjust this setting. Quality refers to the amount of compression used to store your photo, so a low-quality photo takes up less room but has more compression.

The Motorola DROID gives an extra option to change your scene mode. The choices are **Auto**, **Action**, **Portraits**, **Landscape**, **Night**, **Beach**, **Snow**, and **Sunset**. This has to do with your lighting conditions. The Nexus One running Android 2.2 offers exposure settings, as shown in Figure 9–5. Higher numbers make your picture lighter, and lower numbers make your picture darker. This is the equivalent of under- or overexposing film. This is especially useful when you want to take photos of backlit subjects or sunsets.

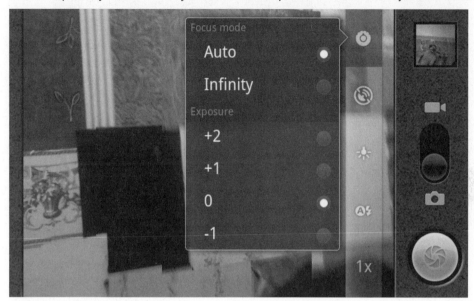

Figure 9–5. *Exposure in Android 2.2*

The focus mode gives you the choice of autofocus or fixed focus. On Android 2.2, these are called "auto" and "infinity" (Figure 9–5), but the meaning is the same. Some phones also offer a macro setting for closeups. If you find that your photos are usually blurry, try adjusting your focus settings.

Shooting Video

If your phone is capable of shooting video, you can change the camera from still-picture to video mode in Android 2.1 and above by sliding the selector on the right upward to the video camera icon. This is shown in Figure 9–6. You'll notice right away that the shutter button at the lower right turns into a video button with a red dot in the middle to start the recording.

Click the button to start recording, and press it again to stop recording. The button will change to show a square VCR-style stop symbol in the middle to indicate that you're recording, and you'll see an overlay of the time elapsed on the lower-right side of the screen.

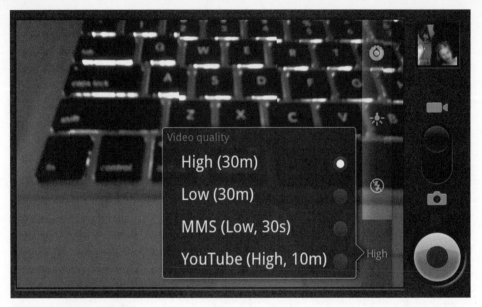

Figure 9–6. *Video recording*

Just as with still photos, you can slide out the preferences tray on the left in Android 2.1 and below, or use the buttons on the right for Android 2.2. For the Nexus One, those options include

1. *Video quality*: Choose "high" for videos you want to upload to YouTube or edit on your desktop, and choose "low" for videos you want to send as MMS messages.

2. *Video duration*: By default this is set to 10 minutes, the maximum length for most YouTube accounts. You can set it to 30 seconds for sending MMS video, and you can set it to 30 minutes. Be careful if you set it to 30 minutes, because that will eat up a lot of space on your phone's storage card.

3. *White balance*: Just as with still images, this lets you override the automatic light settings. Use this if you notice your video is yellow in incandescent lighting or has other color balance issues.

4. *Color effect*: Just as with still photos, this lets you apply color filters to your video. Be aware that you can't unapply a filter, but you can use third-party tools to apply filters later if you need them.

On Android 2.2, you can also use the flash while shooting video. In this case, the flash will stay on during the recording and give your subject a bit of lighting.

You may have also noticed that the preview photo in the upper-right corner changes when you switch to video mode. You can use this to review the last video you took. The review mode is similar to that for still pictures, but instead of a "Set as" button you have a Play button, since videos can't be used as wallpaper or contact icons.

The Gallery

Photos taken from your camera are stored on your phone's memory card, and you can review these using your Camera app. However, you might also have photos you've moved or downloaded from other sources. As discussed in Chapter 8, you can use a file-browsing app to see and copy these files, but it's easier to visually browse them using the Gallery app, as shown in Figure 9–7.

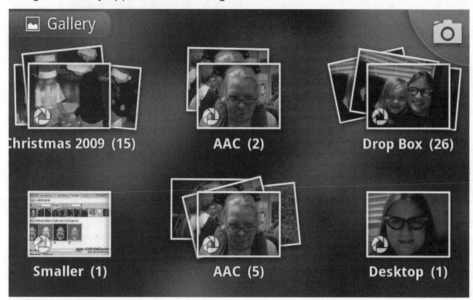

Figure 9–7. *The Gallery app*

The Gallery app is built into Android phones. In earlier versions of Android, the graphics weren't quite as fancy, but the concept was the same. You see a visual representation of pictures you have stored both on your phone and through Google's Picasa Web Albums. Launch the Gallery app to browse your photos.

On phones with Android 2.1 and above, like the Nexus One and DROID, the gallery lets you browse through your pictures by flicking your fingers through the grouped piles of photos. You can browse in either horizontal or vertical mode, and the pictures will realign themselves to match your orientation.

Photos in the gallery can either come from your phone's storage or from Picasa. You'll see an icon to indicate the source, including folders, the camera folder, and Picasa albums. In Figure 9–7, all the pictures on the screen came from Picasa, as indicated by the white Picasa logo on the corner of each album.

Press on an album to view the pictures within it. In Android 2.2 you can also peek into an album without opening it by using the pinch-to-zoom motion. Figure 9–8 shows pictures within an album. You can view pictures in either stack or grid mode. Use the toggle in the upper-right corner of the screen to switch between modes. Grid mode shows all the pictures in an album, while stack mode groups the pictures by the date and time they were taken. You can flick through the pictures in the album with your finger or use the scroll button on the bottom of the screen.

Figure 9–8. *Gallery details*

Click an individual picture to view it, as shown in Figure 9–9.

Figure 9–9. *Viewing a picture*

When you're viewing an individual picture, notice breadcrumbs at the top left, which show you where the picture is located and how many other pictures are in the album. Also notice the zoom options in the upper-right corner. At the bottom of the screen is an option to play a slideshow of all the photos in the current album, and a Menu button. In this case, the Menu button does exactly the same thing as pressing your phone's physical Menu button, and it offers options that are very similar to what you'd see when reviewing pictures through the Camera app. You'll see sharing options, and a More button for cropping, rotating, and viewing the photo on a map. If the photo is stored on your phone, you'll also see a button to delete it.

NOTE: You can upload or delete multiple photos at once through the gallery by viewing an album and pressing the Menu button twice. Gray check marks will appear on each photo or video. Select multiple items by pressing each one. You can then mass-delete them with the Delete button, or upload them to Picasa or YouTube using the Share button.

Using Picasa

Picasa is Google's online and desktop photo software, and it is the default photo service for unmodified Android phones. It is one of your choices when using the Share button, and it provides an easy way to upload a photo for embedding into a web page.

Technically, Picasa and Picasa Web Albums are two separate products, but the distinction is fuzzy, since you can sync online and desktop photos. Picasa Web Albums is located on the Web at http://picasaweb.google.com.

Think of Picasa Web Albums as Google's answer to Flickr. You can upload photos and organize them into albums. Each album can have privacy settings, captions, tags, and location information (geotags). When using the service in a standard web browser, it also has facial recognition capabilities. So far this hasn't been translated into the phone version, but it's only a matter of time. The Xperia X10 has facial recognition software built into it, so it's not a stretch to imagine other phones will follow suit.

Picasa doesn't provide unlimited storage. At the time of publication, it provides 1GB of free storage, and anything beyond that must be purchased from Google on an annual basis.

There are three basic privacy levels for Picasa:

1. *Public*: This is just as it sounds. Your album is visible to anyone and can be found in search.

2. *Unlisted*: Google will give you an obscure URL, which you can distribute as you see fit. This is not actually private; it's just hard to guess. However, anyone with the URL can see your album and pass that URL on to other people, so it is a poor security setting for anything you really need to remain private.

3. *Sign-in Required*: You specify who can see the album. You enter the name of specific users' Google accounts, and only those people can see your album, and only when they are logged in. You can add and remove anyone from your "shared with" list.

To upload a photo to Picasa, click the Share button when viewing a picture in the Gallery app or reviewing a picture in the Camera app. Select Picasa, choose a Google account, enter a caption, and select an album. You can also create an album by pressing the + button next to the drop-down menu, but your only sharing options are Public or Unlisted when you create the album from your phone. Once you've selected the settings, click the Upload button.

Sharing Photos

Picasa is the default option for web albums, but it certainly isn't the only option. You can share photos using Gmail, Email, and MMS messaging, or using a paired Bluetooth device for Bluetooth-capable phones. On many phones, Facebook sharing is also included by default.

You can share photos using any app that includes sharing capabilities, as shown in Figure 9–10. When you view a photo in the Gallery app or review a photo in the Camera app, you'll see the Share button. Clicking the Share button shows you the sharing options for every installed app with that capability.

Figure 9–10. *Sharing*

Using Photos As Wallpaper and Widgets

You can use a photo as your Home screen wallpaper. When you've shot a photo, you can set this immediately, but you can also use photos stored on your phone's card. One method in Android 2.1 and above is to long-click the Home screen, select Wallpapers, and then select Gallery. Navigate to the photo you want to use. You'll see an outline around part of the photo indicating where it will be cropped to fit as your wallpaper. Drag your finger to expand, shrink, or move the cropping area. Click Save when you are done.

Another method is to approach from the other direction and go to the Gallery first. Find the photo you want to use and click Menu ➤ More ➤ "Set as" ➤ Wallpaper. You'll be prompted to go through the same cropping process.

To set a photo as a Picture Frame widget, as shown in Figure 9–11, you can long-click the Home screen, select Widgets, and then select Picture Frame. This will prompt you to browse through the Gallery and find an appropriate photo. In Android 2.2, you can choose how to crop the photo, although it will show you a square cropping area for what will end up being a rectangular frame.

Figure 9–11. *Picture frame*

The advantage of using a widget is that you can display the photo without obscuring it with apps. However, it still takes up space on your Home screen, and in Android 2.1 and 2.2 there's no way to adjust the size of a picture frame or have it rotate through multiple photos without using a third-party app.

Using Photos for Contact Icons

In Chapter 4, I discussed adding personal pictures for your contacts by editing the contact page. You can also add contact photos by browsing to the photo in the Gallery and clicking Menu ➤ More ➤ "Set as," and then clicking the Contact icon. You'll be given the option to crop the image, just as you are for wallpaper. Browse to the contact you want to replace (this is easiest if you use your trackball to scroll through your contacts, so you can avoid accidentally selecting the wrong one). Select the correct contact, and then click Save.

This option is also available immediately after shooting a photo through the "Set as" button, so when you enter a new client or business partner's contact information into your phone, take a quick picture of them and add their picture to the contact info.

Copying Photos to Your Computer

You can get photos from your phone to your computer in many different ways. The method you use depends on the bandwidth you have available, your privacy concerns with the photos, and your personal style. You can e-mail photos to yourself or upload them to Picasa and download them to your desktop from the Web. This may present privacy issues if the photos are sensitive, and it may just take too long if you've taken a lot of photos.

Most Android phones come with some sort of USB connector for recharging and data connection. Connect the USB device to your computer. Windows and Mac computers should automatically install the proper drivers to handle this. However, on the Android side, you need to click your notification tray where it says "USB Connected," and then confirm that you want to mount your phone's media card. The reason you need to confirm this is because you can't use your phone to access your card when it is mounted, which means you can't use the Camera or Gallery app.

You can use your mounted card just like any other USB-connected removable media. Once you've finished copying your photos and videos to your desktop, unmount the drive using the same procedure you would for any other removable media. Next, drag down the notifications panel from the top of the screen and select Turn off USB Storage. Now you can safely remove your USB cable from your phone and computer.

Uploading to YouTube

When you create videos, the primary way to upload and share them is through YouTube. This works really well for personal videos, but it's a bit trickier for corporate videos, because each YouTube "channel" is limited to one user account and one password. Eventually, there may be an easy way to upload to a collaborative channel. Google is currently experimenting with methods to allow users to upload submissions to another channel.

YouTube offers unlimited storage for videos and two basic privacy settings, private and public. Private videos can be shared with small groups of other users. You can also upload videos privately at first and make them public later. Public videos are searchable and are automatically closed-captioned using speech-to-text technology.

Videos on YouTube are limited to 10 minutes unless you are part of YouTube's Partner Program for commercial content creators. More information on YouTube's Partner Program is available at www.youtube.com/t/partnerships_faq.

In order to upload videos to YouTube, you must have a YouTube account, and it must be linked to a Google account. You also have to be using a Wi-Fi connection. It's simply too much to upload on a 3G network, and Android 2.1 will refuse to even try. Android 2.2 will let you do it, but it will still take a long time and use a lot of bandwidth.

You can upload from the Gallery app by viewing the album that contains the video and double-clicking the Menu button. Click the video or videos, and then click Share and select YouTube. Choose an account, a title, a description, tags, and whether you want the video to be public or private; then click Upload.

> **NOTE:** When you give public photos and videos tags and descriptions, keep search in mind. Use terms that you think people searching for that video would use, and do not skip fields.

Editing Photos

Default Android settings give you a few options for editing videos, such as cropping or rotating the picture, and you can adjust the white balance for certain lighting conditions. But what if you want to add an effect after you've already taken the photo or edit out red eye? Fear not, there are tons of apps that allow you to edit photos directly from your phone. Nothing offers the same quality you'd get from a desktop photo-editing program, but you're using this with a phone camera, not the latest SLR.

Photoshop Mobile

Adobe Photoshop is probably the most trusted name in photo-editing software, and Adobe has expanded to also offer a mobile version of its product, as shown in Figure 9–12. It's not nearly as full featured as the desktop version, but it is considerably cheaper. The current price is free.

Figure 9–12. *Photoshop Mobile*

Photoshop Mobile doesn't let you take new photos from within the program, but it lets you work with the photos you already have. Think of it as a Gallery app alternative. It allows you to edit a variety of photos features, including soft focus, saturation, tint, cropping, and color effects. You can upload photos to a free Photoshop.com account (you'll be prompted to create account if you don't have one already).

Once your photos have been uploaded, you can share and edit them from your Photoshop.com account.

PicSay

PicSay is probably the best known of several photo-editing apps that allow you to make artistic and novel changes to photos before uploading them, as shown in Figure 9–13. PicSay comes in a free trial version and a paid app (about $4.00 as I write this). Google Checkout will convert the currency if you buy the app through the Android Market. The trial version of PicSay has an older version of the interface than the for-pay version, and limits the size of pictures. The pro version also offers more editing options.

Figure 9–13. *PicSay*

PicSay allows you to apply an impressive amount of effects to photos. Not only does it allow you to make whimsical edits like applying fake mustaches or novelty eyeballs, but it has an impressive list of very practical effects. You can use it to edit out red-eye, add captions, or add grain and other textures to photos.

Similar photo-editing apps include Pic Paint and Camera Illusion.

Other Photo Apps

If you prefer not to use Picasa for your online photo albums, you can use Photobucket, Flickr, or Facebook, so long as you have a compatible app installed. You can also share photos using Bump, an app that allows you to exchange contact info by physically bumping the phone of another user. Bump was previously an iPhone-only app, but it is now cross-platform compatible with Android users.

Android allows developers to have access to camera controls, so many apps allow you to take photos or use the camera. Price comparison software like ShopSavvy and Compare Everywhere use the camera to scan bar codes. Evernote allows you to take and attach snapshots to notes. Camera Pro and Snap Photo Pro are paid apps that offer higher-end camera features like a timer and grid marks for easier photo composition. Camera Pro even offers to replace the Camera app as the default camera.

Google launched an experimental app for searching with pictures, called Goggles. Goggles is best when used to scan man-made objects like DVD covers, text, and famous buildings. Goggles analyzes any photo you take with it and attempts to identify the object and find it in search. If it can't identify the object, it looks for visually similar images.

Goggles is currently not much more than a novelty, but in the future it may end up being an easier way to search than typing search terms into your phone.

Printing

If you want to print photos, documents, or other files without downloading them to your PC first, you can use the PrinterShare app from the Android Market. Download the free Mac or PC desktop component from http://printershare.com, and install the Android app on your phone. This lets you share that computer's printer access. You can use a trial version to make sure it's compatible with your network and do some limited printing. The $4.95 pro Android app allows you to print directly to Wi-Fi printers and doesn't have a page limit.

Remember that the resolution on most Android cameras is still only enough for quality 5×7-inch prints or smaller.

Summary

The camera phone continues to grow as technology improves. Although commercial point-and-shoot cameras offer better resolution and more storage, the cameras on most new Android phones are not huge sacrifices. You can take decent photos and upload them to photo-sharing sites like Picasa, Flickr, and Facebook. You can also use editing software to enhance images before sharing or even printing directly from your phone. Android also allows you to create and upload YouTube videos.

Because Android allows so much customization in hardware and software, the exact options available on your Android phone will depend on the phone model and carrier.

Chapter 10

Web Browsing

One of the big reasons to own a smartphone is to browse the Web. However, even with the fastest of phones and best of connections, browsing the Web is made complicated by the size of your screen and web designers that didn't take mobile browsers into account. In this chapter, we'll explore ways to get the most from the Web using your Android phone, including use of Android's web browser, alternative browsers, and apps that make browsing faster. We'll also discuss sharing your wireless connection with your laptop.

Before discussing Android specifically, it's helpful to know a little about browsing the Web on mobile devices in general. Web pages are usually designed for screens four times as big as those on a mobile browser, and they don't always take low-speed connections into account. Connection speed may not be a problem if you're connected to Wi-Fi or using a 4G network, but when traveling, you'll often run into slow spots and areas with low cell tower coverage. Web pages designed for desktops can end up taking an eternity to load over an EDGE connection.

To get around this problem, web developers created the WAP (Wireless Access Protocol) standard. WAP sites are designed to load quickly and display well on small screens. You can see an example by visiting Wapedia at `http://wapedia.mobi` on either your phone or desktop browser. Wapedia is a WAP version of Wikipedia.

WAP sites must be intentionally designed, and not every website takes the time to consider mobile devices. On top of that, the WAP version often loses design elements and functionality in favor of quicker loading times. So there are times when viewing a standard website is either desirable or unavoidable.

Android's Web Browser

Android's web browser is a major part of the Android platform. It can be run as the Browser app or embedded as a feature in other apps. The Browser app is based on the same core technology that powers the iPhone's web browser, WebKit. Apple developed WebKit for use in their Safari web browser, and then later released the code as open source.

WebKit is also used in alternative browsers for Android, like Skyfire and Dolphin. Google uses WebKit for both Android's Browser app and Chrome, its desktop web browser.

Anatomy of a Browser

You can launch Android's web browser through the Browser app. In Android 2.2, the Browser app is at the bottom of the screen, on the right side of the app tray, as shown in Figures 10–6 and 10–8. Initially when you launch the Browser app, you'll see a screen that resembles Figure 10–1.

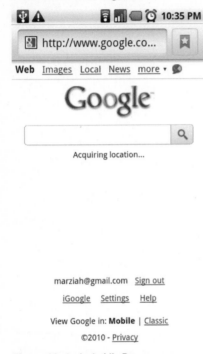

Figure 10–1. *Android's Browser app*

The Browser app does not use tabs for navigation. Instead, the top of the browser shows the current URL and has a bookmarking tool to the right of the URL. The rest of the area renders web pages similarly to most web browsers. However, if a website detects that you're using a mobile browser, you'll generally see a version optimized for mobile devices.

Browser is location aware. That means that Browser can hook into location services on your phone to determine where you are. That might be useful if you want to find local search results or coupons, or it may seem like an invasion of privacy. In order to mitigate this concern, each website must ask permission to determine your location, and you can revoke that permission at any time. I'll discuss how you do that later in this chapter.

Basic Navigation

Scrolling is done by simply touching the page and moving it with a finger. If you're viewing the mobile version of a web page, such as Google's mobile page in Figure 10–1, the entire page will be sized appropriately for your screen, so you won't need to zoom in and out. If you're viewing a standard web page, you might find that you need to view things a little closer.

The first thing to remember is that viewing pages horizontally is an option. Most phones auto-rotate, but some models with physical keyboards require you to slide out the keyboard to force horizontal orientation. If you find this to be annoying, you can use Droidsans Virtual Keyboard instead. Oftentimes it's easier to scroll up and down on a page than it is to scroll side to side. If you're using a device that supports it, you can zoom out by using a pinching motion with two fingers and zoom in by using a reverse-pinching motion (as if pulling the page corners outward with two fingers).

If you're using an older device or can't use both fingers, you can also expand and contract pages by pressing once on the page, and then clicking the + and – magnifying glass buttons that appear in the bottom-right corner of the screen, as shown in Figure 10–2.

Figure 10–2. *Zooming*

NOTE: Although multitouch capability was included in the very first commercial Android release, Google didn't turn on the capability by default until Android 2.1. The result may have been one of the reasons Apple launched a patent infringement lawsuit against HTC in 2010. The suit is seen by many analysts as a proxy lawsuit against Google.

Navigating Multiple Windows

The Browser app doesn't use tabs, so sometimes you're faced with navigating more than one open window. To see a list of all open windows and switch between them, press the Menu button, and then click the Windows option. Figure 10–3 shows a list of open windows. In order to switch to a new active window, just click it. In order to close a window, click the X next to it. If you ever find Browser's performance is slowing down, you may want to check to see if you have unnecessary windows open that you can close.

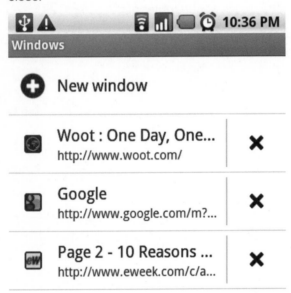

Figure 10–3. *Active windows*

Alternatively, if you're on a page you don't want to leave, you can press the Menu button and choose "New window" to keep the current page active and launch a new active window.

Bookmarks

You can navigate to any web page by clicking the address bar and entering a URL, but navigating by bookmark is more efficient. Create a bookmark by clicking the star to the right of the address bar. You'll see a page similar to Figure 10–4. Click the Add square to add your new bookmark. You'll be given a chance to confirm the URL and change the name of the bookmark if you like. The default is the title set by the web designer.

Figure 10–4. *Bookmarks*

You can navigate back through your bookmarks by pressing the Menu button and then clicking Bookmarks. You can also switch from thumbnail view to list view by pressing the Menu button again while viewing your bookmarks.

You may notice that your bookmark collection has been prepopulated with common sites like Wikipedia and MSN. If you want to get rid of a bookmark you'll never visit, long-click the bookmark and select "Delete bookmark."

Long-clicking a bookmark also gives you quite a few other options. You can use a bookmarked page as your default home page, or create a shortcut on your Home screen. You can also share the bookmark over Twitter, Facebook, Delicious, Gmail, SMS messaging, or any other installed app that has this feature enabled. If sharing directly is not possible, you can copy the URL through a long-click as well.

NOTE: Bookmarks are not backed up or shared with your desktop browser. If you need to upgrade phones or perform a hard reset, you will lose your bookmarks.

Most Visited and History

When you view your bookmarks, you may notice that you have two other tabs, "Most visited" and History. The History tab is shown in Figure 10–5. This lets you navigate through the pages you've visited often or recently, and it can be a real time saver. Rather than having to browse to your favorite page repeatedly, you can view it in your history or most-visited pages and click the star next to the address to instantly add it to your bookmark collection.

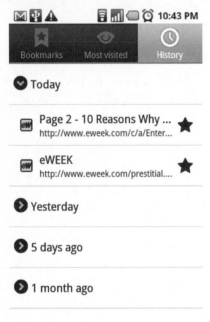

Figure 10–5. *History*

When browsing your history, you'll also notice that sites are divided by how long ago you visited them. Today's sites are shown by default, but other dates are hidden. Open the list for other time ranges by clicking the round button next to the date range.

Adding Bookmarks to Your Home Screen

As mentioned, you can long-click a bookmark to add it to your Home screen as a shortcut. It will be added to whichever page on that screen you viewed directly before launching Browser.

If you want to go in the other direction, long-click the Home screen where you want to add a shortcut, as shown in Figure 10–6; select Shortcuts, and then Bookmark; and then browse to the bookmark you want to add. Adding shortcuts to your Home screen is a quick way to add frequently visited sites that don't have their own app.

Figure 10–6. *Adding shortcuts to the Home screen*

Searching the Web

One of the most common reasons to use the Web on your phone is so you can search the Web, and that's how Google's search handles your request. In most installations of Android, there's a search widget already installed on your phone. The default search engine is, of course, Google. You can click the Quick Search widget and enter a search term using text. Click the magnifying glass, and your phone will show your search results, as shown in Figure 10–7. Strictly speaking, this isn't actually the Browser app. However, clicking any link will launch your browser.

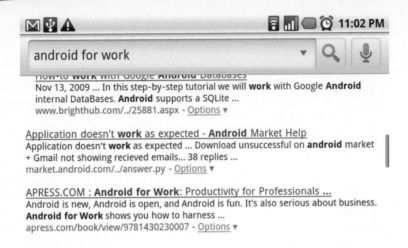

Figure 10–7. *Searching*

TIP: Are you afraid you'll accidentally find inappropriate search results at work? Whenever you're looking at search results in Android 2.1, you can press the Menu button and then click Settings. You'll be able to adjust Google's SafeSearch settings. By default, it is set to moderate filtering. You can switch this to strict if you're worried, or just turn it off entirely if you're not. SafeSearch is designed to filter out profanity, pornography, explicit sexual content, and hate language. There's never any guarantee you won't find something offensive that manages to evade the filter, but it's a reasonable precaution in many work environments.

Voice Search

What if you want to search, but don't have the time or room to do all the typing for your search terms? The Google Quick Search widget is also a voice search widget. Just click the microphone icon next to the text box and speak when prompted, as shown in Figure 10–8. Google will attempt to interpret what you say and search as if you'd typed in text.

Now, this process isn't perfect by any stretch. It won't work well in noisy environments, and it doesn't always interpret exotic words. For example, trying to search for "Marziah" usually ends up launching a search for "Malaysia." However, "Barbecue in Kansas City" is a search that usually gets results.

Figure 10–8. *Voice search*

> **NOTE:** Not only does searching for a nearby restaurant or business do well with voice search, it
> highlights another feature of Android's Browser app: it will attempt to find and interpret phone
> numbers and locations. If you press down on any text-based phone number, the Dialer app will
> launch with that phone number already entered in, ready to call. If you press on a location, Maps
> will launch to find the spot.

Searching Within Results

If you're searching for a specific piece of information in a long page of text, it's very
helpful to know exactly where you should look.

On your computer desktop, you might use Google's cached file to find your keywords.
They'll show up highlighted on the page. You can do that with Android's Browser app.
Just click the More link after each search result, and you can search for similar pages,
mobile-formatted pages, or cached images when available.

Another way to find what you need quickly is to search within the page itself. When
you're looking at a web page, press the physical Search button on your phone, and
you'll search within that page. Your keywords will highlight as you're typing them, as
shown in Figure 10–9.

Figure 10–9. *Searching within a page*

Browser Settings

You have quite a bit of control over your browser experience. From within Browser, press the physical Menu button, then press More, and then Settings, and you'll see the settings page, as shown in Figure 10–10. There are roughly two pages of settings in Android 2.1.

Some of the more important ones include the default page zoom. Adjust this to fit your eyesight and preferences. You can also specify web pages to *always* display horizontally and choose to shrink pages down for better phone display. If bandwidth is an issue in your area, you can also opt not to display pictures at all by unchecking the box next to "Load images."

There are also security choices. You can choose to have the Browser app remember form data and store passwords. Technically, it is more secure to not store your password within the browser, but if you already use a security lock on your phone, storing the passwords might be a necessary evil to avoid the frustration of having to reenter passwords on your phone—especially secure passwords with capital letters, punctuation, and numbers.

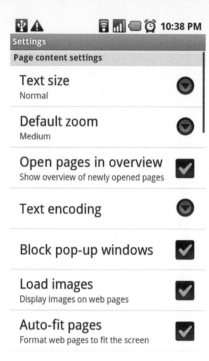

Figure 10–10. *Page content settings*

The settings here also allow you to give location data to web sites that ask for it. This can help you out for finding local restaurants in search results or entering location data when you make a blog entry. However, you must approve location requests on a per-web site basis, and you can revoke them by clicking "Clear location access." Clear individual location permissions by clicking "Website settings" in the Advanced Settings section.

You can also allow JavaScript and browser plug-ins. While Android supports plug-ins, at this point the list of available plug-ins is pretty short. Allowing plug-ins is also an all-or-nothing deal at this time, but as the Browser app becomes more sophisticated, that may change.

Flash

Adobe Flash is available for Android 2.2 and above as a download from the Android Market. You can use Bsquare's Flash Lite on Android 1.5 to play most videos, or you can use Skyfire's alternative web browser in Android 2.1.

For the most part, the absence of Flash doesn't feel like a huge loss. Other than digital video, Flash is mainly used for serving advertising. You can't play Flash-based web games on Android 2.1 and below, but most phones are not fast enough to really do it justice if you could.

Alternative Browsers

You're not stuck waiting for the Browser app to develop a feature or fix an issue. Third parties are free to develop their own web browsers, and many of them have. You can even specify that an alternative browser be your default browser, just like you can on your desktop computer by checking a box in your browser's settings. If you've installed more than one browser, Android will also ask you to choose which browser you want to use for each action until you select one as your default browser.

Next, we'll go over some of the more popular alternatives to the Browser app.

Opera Mini

The first alternative browser I'll discuss is Opera Mini, which is shown in Figure 10–11.

Figure 10–11. *Opera Mini*

Opera offers browsers for a lot of portable devices, including game consoles, netbooks, and phones. If you're an Opera user, you can share your bookmarks across devices. Opera speeds up page-load times by precompressing them through Opera's servers. However, because every page viewed through Opera Mini has to go through a proxy and potentially be reformatted, your viewing experience may not be as good as it is on Android's Browser app. Experiment to see if the quicker speed makes other sacrifices worth it.

Dolphin

One of the most popular alternative browsers for Android is Dolphin, shown in Figure 10–12. It's also my favorite. Dolphin is WebKit based, like the Browser app, and it supports multitouch pinch-to-zoom gestures. It also allows for tabbed browsing instead of having to use the Menu button and find open windows.

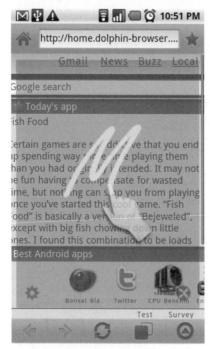

Figure 10–12. *Dolphin gestures*

Dolphin supports plug-ins, and, unlike the Browser app, allows you to manage plug-ins individually through the Settings menu. Developers have caught on, and there are many plug-ins and themes available for Dolphin.

One of the coolest features of Dolphin is gesture support. Click the gesturing hand in the bottom-right corner of the screen (you can change this location in the settings), and you can use preconfigured or user-defined gestures to navigate. For instance, trace *M* to add a bookmark, or add your own gesture to navigate to Google.

Users of phones with Android 2.0 and above can download Dolphin Browser HD for even more options, including a "thumbnail-flick" menu, which lets you browse through favorites and tabs by flicking side to side, and the ability to back up your bookmarks to your SD card and download YouTube videos for smoother viewing.

One of the more user-friendly features I appreciate is that Dolphin Browser HD launches a tutorial the very first time you use it and prompts you to change your default browser and install a shortcut to your Home screen.

Dolphin HD's biggest disadvantage is the same reason it won't run on older versions of Android: it's resource intensive. If you find your browser slowing down, switch to the standard version of Dolphin Browser.

Skyfire

Skyfire's biggest advantage is that it allows you to play Flash movies in versions of Android that won't support Adobe's official Flash app. In order for this to work, it goes through a proxy server to render out the video. It's similar to what Opera Mini does in order to precompress web pages.

Not all video works for Skyfire, because not all Flash video sites have gone through Skyfire's servers. Skyfire's home screen lists sites with supported video, and the collection is pretty impressive. Skyfire still works as a substitute for full Flash support on phones that don't support Adobe's app. You may want to hold off on using it as your default browser, though, because both Dolphin Browser and the Browser app support more standard web browsing features.

Steel

If you're having problems with the Browser app taking up too much storage space with cached files, you might check out Steel. Steel is designed to be a minimalist version of the standard Browser app, and runs on Android 1.5 and above.

Tethering and Portable Hotspots

Let's say you choose none of the above for your web browsing. You can use Android phones as portable modems to let you connect your laptop or netbook to the Internet. This process is called *tethering*, or sometimes referred to as creating a *portable hotspot* when a USB cable is not required.

Before we proceed, I will caution you to check with your phone carrier. Not all carriers allow you to tether your phone, and most charge extra for the privilege. Android 2.2 supports USB tethering and creating a portable hotspot, and newer phones like the HTC EVO, which aren't running Android 2.2, have added tethering options, although Sprint does charge for the privilege.

Creating Portable Hotspots in Android 2.2

If you have an Android 2.2 phone, it's easy to share your signal with your laptop. The process is similar on an HTC EVO.

1. From the Home screen, press the Menu button.

2. Select Wireless & Networks.

3. Select "Tethering & portable hotspot." You should see a screen similar to Figure 10–13.

 Tethering or hotspot active

Tethering & portable hotspot

USB tethering
USB connected, check to tether

Portable Wi-Fi hotspot
Portable hotspot AndroidAP active

Portable Wi-Fi hotspot settings
Set up & manage portable Wi-Fi hotspot

Help

Figure 10–13. *Tethering in Android 2.2*

4. Click the box next to either "USB tethering" or "Portable Wi-Fi hotspot."

You can also save a few of these steps by using the QuickTeth app. It's a simple widget that allows you to go directly to step 4.

If you are using your phone as a portable hotspot, you can connect to it as if it were just another Wi-Fi hotspot. However, that means everyone else could connect to your hotspot, too. In the interest of both security and conserving your bandwidth, you'll want to set a password.

To configure your settings, click the Portable Wi-Fi hotspot settings link, and then click "Configure Wi-Fi hotspot." You'll see a screen similar to Figure 10–14.

Figure 10–14. *Wi-Fi settings*

From here, you can change your SSID (service set identifier)—that is, the name of the hotspot you'll see in your laptop's list of available networks. In standard Android 2.2, you only have two security options: Open and WPA2 PSK. Needless to say, Open is not the secure option. With this option, anyone who sees your network can use it. WPA2 PSK (Wi-Fi Protected Access 2, Pre-Shared Key) is an Internet standard for personal hotspots that lets you password-lock your network. Select this option, and then enter a password. If no one is looking over your shoulder, click the "Show password" option to avoid fat-fingering issues. Click Save when you're done, and then use your laptop to connect as if it were a regular Wi-Fi hotspot.

When your phone is being used as a hotspot, you'll see an icon in the notification bar at the top of the screen to let you know. You can turn off your hotspot by clicking it in the notification bar and then deselecting "Portable Wi-Fi hotspot."

Just because you don't need to plug your phone in with a USB cable to use it as a modem doesn't mean it's not a good idea. Portable hotspots use a lot of battery juice, and plugging in the USB keeps it charged as you go.

Tethering in Android 2.1 and Earlier

If you search Google for "Android tethering," you'll find a lot of solutions that say you need to "root" your phone. What they're referring to is gaining superuser administrative access to your phone. This is a risky procedure involving some serious hacking, and it's not something I'd recommend attempting. There's a chance you could accidentally break your phone in the process. Fortunately, there are at least two methods for tethering that don't involve rooting your phone.

Proxoid is a free app that allows you to tether without having to root your phone. However, the installation is complicated and involves downloading and modifying the Android SDK (Software Developer's Kit). The instructions are here: `http://code.google.com/p/proxoid/wiki/installationPhone`. Be sure to also click the platform-specific instructions.

A less complicated method is using a paid app like PdaNet (see Figure 10–15) or EasyTether. Generally, these apps require you to install software on both your laptop and the phone, so this isn't something that will work if you aren't authorized to install software. However, it comes with a free trial to make sure you've installed everything correctly. You can either use your USB cable or Bluetooth connection. Of the two, the USB option is faster. It also keeps your phone charged. However, it tends to run hot when tethering, so be sure to keep your phone well ventilated.

Figure 10–15. *PdaNet*

PdaNet costs a one-time $24 fee. It includes a widget for turning tethering on and off from your Home screen. EasyTether is a similar app for $10.05 with a sample version EasyTether Lite. Either app potentially pays for itself with a single stay at a hotel that doesn't provide free Wi-Fi.

Summary

Android's Browser app is a standards-compliant web browser designed for mobile. To make up for the smaller screen size, Android removes the tabs and adds the ability to interpret phone numbers and locations. If you'd rather have the tabs, you can use Dolphin or Skyfire. In the future, you'll also be able to use Firefox for Android, which Mozilla recently announced that it is developing.

You can also tether your phone's data access to your laptop and browse the Web with a full-sized browser, although you will need to check with your phone carrier's terms of service to see if this is acceptable use.

Chapter 11

Social Media and Work

What is social media? Social media can broadly be defined as Internet sites and apps designed around social interaction. I could argue that the Internet has always been a social invention, but instead I'll tell you the story of when I attended a friend's birth shower several years ago. I'd met this friend online, even though she lived in the same town, and at one point during the party, everyone in the room introduced themselves by name—and LiveJournal username. LiveJournal was a blogging/social networking service that predated MySpace and Facebook. I'm used to people my age socializing electronically, but when the grandmother-to-be also introduced herself by LiveJournal username, I knew social networks weren't just something kids used to find dates.

The moment I realized that business was finally catching on to this whole social media phenomena was when I was on Twitter and mentioned that I was pondering what to do with some domain names I'd registered. One of the companies I mentioned was obviously monitoring Twitter and offered me a coupon to stay with them within minutes of my post. This company's domain hosting cost a little more even with a coupon, but I used the coupon and stayed with them because I knew they were paying attention to customer feedback. Who could beat that level of customer service?

These days, being social can be good business. It's become a regular portion of CRM (customer relationship management). Keep your customers updated with your latest projects, keep them excited about your products and services, and let them tell you where you should go next. Social media also helps you personally network with your colleagues or find your next opportunity.

Social media done badly can also be bad business for you or your company, so make sure you understand and follow any policies your business may have about Internet posting. People have been fired for casual posts they've made on their blog, Facebook, Twitter, and other social media web sites.

In this chapter, we'll explore some of the social media tools available for Android, and how you can make efficient use of your social time both on and off the clock.

Twitter and Microblogs

Twitter is part of a new generation of short, public blogging tools known as *microblog*s. It's a rapidly evolving service that essentially started out as a blog-like public collection of SMS messages from a given user. Twitter posts, or *tweets*, are limited to 140 characters to reflect their start in SMS. However, Twitter is also available from the Web, so many users are not accessing it by their phone at all. Twitter gained popularity in part because it allowed a lot of open use from third-party tools. Some (but not all) of those tools have made their way to Android.

Why would you use Twitter? The short messages are great for keeping status updates. If your business is transportation, let the riders know about delays. If your business is weather dependent, let your customers know if you need to make cancellations. Use it to advertise specials, promote your latest accomplishments, or deepen your customer engagement by having a conversation about their needs. Or just listen to what your customers or colleagues in the industry are saying. Chris Brogan has an excellent blog post on the subject here: `www.chrisbrogan.com/50-ideas-on-using-twitter-for-business`.

The Mechanics and Culture of Twitter

When I explain Twitter at presentations, I tell everyone to think of it like a noisy party where everyone has to speak loudly. As you walk through the party, you can hear snippets of conversations, but you can't always be sure who is being addressed. I'm not the only one to make that observation. In fact, there's an entire book that uses the party analogy: *Social Media Is a Cocktail Party*, by Jim Tobin and Lisa Braziel (CreateSpace, 2008).

The basic mechanics of Twitter are this. Twitter is a free service available at `http://twitter.com`. Every user can make 140-character posts in their own Twitter "stream." You can follow other users and they can follow you. You have a stream of all the posts from people you follow. You can choose to make your stream public or visible to only those you preapprove as followers, but you can't specify privacy on individual posts. The number of followers a person has can be taken as a measure of authority, though it's not an absolute measure. Ashton Kutcher's Twitter account has nearly 5 million followers right now, while the CEO of Google, Eric Schmidt, has just over 80,000.

Many of Twitter's conventions were ad hoc creations designed to work around some of Twitter's shortcomings. Twitter is an unthreaded conversation stream. I can make a post in my stream as a reply to someone else, but my response remains in my Twitter feed, not theirs. In order to indicate replies, people began using the `@username` convention, so replies to me would be `@marziah`, for example. Eventually, Twitter worked this into the system and began making automatic links to users based on this, and letting users know whenever they had a new `@reply` or `@mention`.

Retweets

If someone says something you agree with, like, or want to repeat, you don't repeat it, you *retweet* it. That's a repeat that gives credit to the original author. The convention for retweets is `RT: @username`, followed by the repeated message. Twitter also picked up on this convention and allows you to press a button and retweet messages with the other user's icon to indicate the source. However, some users still opt for the old `RT: @username` style retweets because it allows them to add commentary before the retweet.

Hashtags

Searching for relevant information on a given topic is difficult, so users began putting unlikely character combinations into their posts to tag them or help sort related posts in search. The # (hash) became the common marker for these tags, so the hashtag was born. Sometimes conventions or advertising campaigns mention a particular hashtag, and sometimes the hashtag is spontaneous and viral.

URL Shorteners

Because you've only got 140 characters, you don't have room for long URLs. A new service emerged that would simply forward links from a shorter URL to a longer one. URL shorteners themselves became shorter to save space, so services like TinyURL.com ended up competing with services like bit.ly, ow.ly, and tr.im. Many of these services also added value, such as metrics for the shortened URLs.

> **NOTE:** Avoid using shortened URLs when they're not necessary. Using a shortened URL means that you are relying on a third party to forward your link. That third party could go out of business or have an outage at any time, making you look unprofessional for having a broken link. In fact, this is exactly what happened to tr.im in April of 2010 when they announced that they were going out of the URL shortening business and ceasing all forwards at the end of 2010. Some URLs are also "nicer" than others when it comes to forwarding your links in a way that search engines can easily crawl.

TwitPic

TwitPic was created by Noah Everett to solve the problem of photo sharing on Twitter. It's a separate service, but interconnected. You must register for a TwitPic account at `http://twitpic.com`, but your Twitter username is your TwitPic username, and each photo has its own comment thread on TwitPic. Many phone Twitter apps tie into TwitPic or use similar services, so uploading and linking a photo is a quick process that can be accomplished entirely from your phone.

Direct Messages

Direct messages—or DMs—are short, private messages you can send to a follower that is also following you. They're almost like e-mail message, but you're still constrained to 140 characters. You can send a direct message using a button for that specific purpose.

Finding Twitter Apps

There are many Twitter apps for Android, including the official Twitter app from the Twitter team (which runs on Android 2.1 or higher). That doesn't mean the official app is the best or the only one you should consider. Many third-party apps provide enhanced features.

It may be helpful to make a list of priority features before deciding on an app. Most apps also come with lite and premium options, so you can try before you buy. Some factors in your decision may include

- Support for multiple accounts
- URL shortening
- Link metrics
- Speed
- Ability to upload and link pictures or video
- Ability to create and track custom keyword searches
- List support—both viewing and adding
- Ability to follow, unfollow, and block accounts
- Ability to easily send retweets and direct messages
- Widgets
- Background sync

HootSuite is my personal favorite Twitter app. You can use it to manage multiple accounts, and the interface makes it clear which account is posting. If you buy the premium app, you can also track visitors through its URL-shortening service, ow.ly. Figure 11–1 also shows my favorite feature, scheduled tweets. You can use this to precompose press releases or turn 3:00 a.m. deep thoughts into mid-afternoon topics of conversation. Just press the calendar icon when composing a message and choose when to send it.

Figure 11–1. *HootSuite*

Twidroyd and Touiteur (pronounced *Twitter*) are also two popular apps with both free and paid versions. Twidroyd was formerly known as Twidroid, but TweetUp changed the name when they purchased it to avoid any branding confusion with the LucasArts trademarked term *droid*. They also announced that they'd made deals with handset makers to bundle Twidroyd with future phones.

Touiteur offers nice features like trend search, but you must upgrade to the €1.99 (about $2.60) version to upload pictures or manage multiple accounts. Tweetcaster is a $4.99 app with a pleasant user interface that supports saved searches, so you can keep checking on hashtags and keywords. You can also search for nearby tweets to see what's trending in your local community. Seesmic is a full-featured free app that supports multiple accounts and is also available for desktop computers.

Twitter's official app (shown in Figure 11–2) is easy to use and supports all the official Twitter features, such as lists, and @mentions. It also comes with a nice widget, and it looks fantastic. The splash screen, shown in Figure 11–2, has a bird that flaps its wings and lists trending topics. However, the Twitter app doesn't support multiple accounts, and it only works with Android 2.1 and above.

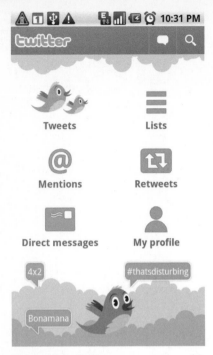

Figure 11–2. *Twitter*

As you find your favorite Twitter app, keep a few things in mind. Nearly all of them allow you to change how often they check for new tweets. Unless you absolutely, positively must be notified of new tweets, turn this to a reasonable, battery-conserving setting of 30 minutes or longer.

Many apps allow you to use either your own URL-shortening service or use theirs. Pick a service that offers you tracking and metrics, even if you don't think you'll use them just yet. It's easier to have the data than it is to wish you had the data.

Yammer

If you want the instant communication of Twitter, but you want to restrict access to your company, you may want to try Yammer (www.yammer.com). Yammer creates a Twitter-like atmosphere that is only accessible to people with the same e-mail domain. Yammer also adds threaded conversations to the tweets and organizational charts, so it has value beyond a simple Twitter imitation. Recently it has also added the ability to create communities across multiple e-mail domains, so it's possible to have a partnership community with vendors and customers.

Yammer makes an official app. It's not robust, but it does allow you to post and see status updates. Fortunately, the intracompany nature of Yammer means that you don't need the same bells and whistles for communication as you would for Twitter.

Other Microblogs

Twitter stole most of the microblog spotlight, but you may prefer a different platform for your message. There's no shortage of microblogging services, so there's no chance I'll name them all. Some, like Jaiku, seem to be short on dedicated apps. Others have a large selection.

Tumblr is worthy of mention. It allows short microblogs posts, but it also supports multimedia better than Twitter by directly embedding it in threads, and allows for threaded responses to posts. There are multiple Android apps that support Tumblr, both free and premium. The free ttTumblr app shown in Figure 11–3 offers a lot of features with a simple user interface.

Figure 11–3. *ttTumblr*

Plurk is another microblogging alternative to Twitter and Facebook. It organizes posts on a timeline and assigns "karma" for participation. Like Tumblr, it allows easier multimedia embedding, and it has built-in privacy settings to make it useful for both small and large groups. Posts are organized on a scrolling horizontal timeline, which allows threaded responses. The Web timeline interface makes it challenging to translate to a phone app, but the app, PlurQ (shown in Figure 11–4), does a good job of attempting it.

Figure 11-4. *PlurQ*

Social Bookmarking

Social bookmarking is a method of sharing sites you like. In the purest form, Delicious, one of the leading social bookmarking services (www.delicious.com), allows you to save a bookmark with a quick note and tags to organize the bookmark by category. You can also network with other users to see their bookmarks and measure the relative popularity of bookmarks by seeing how many other users have marked a particular site.

Instead of using a dedicated Delicious app as a standalone app, use it to enhance your browser. When an app such as Bookmarking for Delicious is installed, it adds an option to the Share page (Menu ➤ More ➤ Share page) from within your Web browser to add bookmarks to your Delicious account.

Digg (http://digg.com) is another widely popular social bookmarking site; unlike Delicious, Digg also adds a threaded comment discussion. Digg emphasizes quantity and focuses on showing the most popular links of the moment as a method of crowd-sourced news. Users can "digg" or "bury" items to see what stories float to the top. Similar services include Reddit and Slashdot. Sites like these can attract huge crowds of visitors to a site, so it makes good business sense for blogs that can handle the traffic to encourage them.

Android apps are available for all three services. You just need to decide how involved you need to be from your phone. Do you need to comment and submit bookmarks, or do you just want to see what the currently trending articles are? Do you want a full app or just a widget?

Facebook

This social network started out as a simple virtual yearbook for college students and has morphed into one of the most popular web sites in the world. As of this publication, it's even more popular than Google search in terms of sheer volume of page views.

Facebook is meant for people to use their actual names instead of pseudonyms, and share information with small to large circles of acquaintance. However, Facebook has been facing increasing scrutiny over its privacy policies and confusing security settings, so when you use Facebook, the wisest course of action, as with any web site, is to assume anything you say is completely visible to the world.

Facebook allows multiple types of posts—from quick status updates to photos, videos, and longer notes. You can also link to articles, videos, and pictures hosted outside of Facebook and add apps that add games, group reading lists, and more. Facebook is also moving toward a universal "Like" button that allows you to interact with pages and web sites outside of Facebook.

How do you manage both personal and business contacts on Facebook? You can do it a couple of ways. One way I *don't* recommend to create multiple accounts. If you create multiple accounts using your real name, it will only serve to confuse you and your contacts when they try to add you as a friend.

The two approaches you can take is are to either friend everyone and assign them to friend groups through the privacy settings, or create a fan page. Fan pages (officially, Facebook just calls them "pages") got their name from the way people used to add them to their feed. They'd "become a fan" of the page. Facebook has changed this mechanism to a simple "Like" button.

Currently Facebook has a 5,000 friend limit on personal accounts, so if you anticipate reaching that limit between clients, fans, and good friends, you need a fan page. Even if you don't anticipate an overwhelming deluge of clients and business contacts friending you, it may still be disturbing to manage personal and work acquaintances in the same social space.

Creating Fan Pages

You set up fan pages through the Ads and Pages application. If you don't have any pages, search for "Ads and Pages" from within Facebook. I'd suggest using a desktop browser to get this set up.

The advantage of using a fan page is that you can make a fan page an official company presence without needing to be friends with any of the fans of the page. The disadvantage is that you do not see the activity fans generate anywhere outside of that page. Whether or not you want your business contacts mingling with your classmates and relatives is a personal decision, but you should decide how you want to handle the situation before you get your first friend request. It's a lot easier to have a separate space established in advance than it is to move everyone over to one later.

> **NOTE:** Whether or not you are Facebook friends with colleagues, business partners, or customers, it's just bad business to badmouth *any* of them. They may not be able to see what you've said, but it's not hard to copy and paste. The last thing you need is for casual gossip to get back to the victim. People have been fired for less.

Facebook Apps

Because Facebook is so enormously popular, chances are your phone already shipped with a decent Facebook app. If not, you can download the official Facebook app for free, or one of many competing Facebook apps, such as Facebook Touch. Figure 11–5 shows the official Facebook app and widget. Facebook's official app is great for personal networking. You can also use it to sync status updates with your contacts, and when the app is installed in Android 2.1 and higher, you can upload photos directly to Facebook from your phone using the photo sharing option covered in Chapter 9.

Figure 11–5. *Facebook widget*

Phones with custom user interfaces offer even more Facebook integration. MOTOBLUR and SenseUI both offer extensive Facebook integration.

Personal Facebook management isn't a problem, but managing fan pages and groups from your phone requires going beyond the default. The easiest method to post directly to fan pages I've found is through Ping.fm. Ping.fm (which is also the URL) is a service that allows you to cross-post to an impressive number of social media sites at once. I'll cover cross-posting at the end of this chapter.

LinkedIn

LinkedIn is a social networking site for professionals. It's designed primarily as a place to hang your resume, cross-network with business partners, give and receive recommendations, and offer status updates about your latest accomplishments. Although it's something you may think of as a tool for job seekers, it's a good idea to build and maintain your network while you aren't looking for work.

Establish yourself as a trusted source in your community by joining groups and recommending colleagues. Chances are you will need to look for work at some point, and it's better to have connections and trust already available now than try to build them out of desperation.

LinkedIn has grown in popularity among business users by adding features for use beyond a simple chart of connections. LinkedIn claims to have more than 65 million users in 200 countries. With that popularity, LinkedIn has also gained features that add appeal beyond job seeking. You can network with colleagues in user groups, add your Twitter feed, and add applications like reading lists and document sharing.

Android doesn't sport an official LinkedIn app as of this publication, and there are only a couple of third-party choices. Linked, by JUPE (shown in Figure 11–6), is an ad-sponsored app that offers basic status updates and reading, allows you to see your contacts, and allows you to search and send contact requests.

Figure 11–6. *Linked*

Blogging

Blogs—short for "weblogs"—started out as a series of manually maintained updates with no ability to comment, but today blogs are a thriving, interactive format used worldwide. Many businesses use blogs to keep customers informed about their products, issue press releases, or just put a human face on their company. Freelancers often keep blogs as a way to self promote. In some cases, the blog itself has become the business, with advertising and market tie-ins generating enough revenue for the blogger to quit their day job.

Since blogs are generally intended to be public and visible, it's vital that you and your boss are clear on your intentions when it comes to corporate blogging. If you maintain a personal blog, it should go without saying, but be careful what you say about your boss or customers, even under a pseudonym.

The standard format for most blogs is that the newest entry goes at the top, with older entries following it. The page itself uses RSS or Atom, two formats for blog aggregation to make it easier for viewers to read the blog or find new updates without having to visit the blog itself. Feeds can be full, partial, or headline only. While full feeds are certainly the most convenient for readers, they also make it easier for content thieves to steal blog entries and claim them as their own.

Phone Posts

Most blog platforms offer a method to e-mail blog entries. Some also offer a way to post blog entries via SMS text message. Some, like LiveJournal, even offer a way to call and voice-record a message. In LiveJournal's case, users can then manually transcribe the voice recording, so you can call in with a quick update (e.g., "It's a girl!" or "Accident on the 435 bridge") without having to enter text.

As Android and smartphones become more popular, blogging platforms have also discovered the value in providing a native phone app for making and managing posts. Blogaway and other third-party apps will support Blogger, though Google hasn't released an official app.

WordPress

WordPress deserves specific mention because it is the most popular blogging platform. It can be used for content management beyond blogging, as well, but blogs are still the main drive. WordPress is open source and free. It can be templated and modified to run on corporate sites, and it can power personal blogs as well. There are a large variety of plug-ins and extensions from both free and premium developers.

WordPress is supported on Android through a native WordPress app, as shown in Figure 11–7. You can post with formatting, tag posts, and geotag posts, and manage comments. You can also add photos and video to your posts.

Figure 11–7. *WordPress*

You aren't offered as many options for templating and administration as you'd see from a desktop browser, but you probably don't *want* as many options when you're trying to type them in on a slide-out keyboard or touchscreen. If you need more access on the road, log into your account from your Android's web browser.

Bump

What if you still want to socially network the old-fashioned way? You still can. Bump (see Figure 11–8) is an app available for both iPhones and Android that allows you to share your contact information by launching the application and then touching another Bump user's phone.

Figure 11–8. *Bump*

Android and iPhone Bump users can share contact info with each other this way as well. You do need a reasonable network connection, since it transmits your information over cell or Wi-Fi networks, not Bluetooth. Android users can share free apps from phone to phone as well.

Buzz

Google has been trying to compete in the social media arena, but so far it hasn't made much progress. One of its latest endeavors is Buzz. Google Buzz is part of Gmail, but it acts like a separate service. Google has been heavily promoting Buzz, so it may end up becoming more popular as a social and self-promotional tool.

Google Buzz allows for long posts that can embed photos and videos, as shown in Figure 11–9. You can create private or public posts and follow the posts of your contacts. Posts in your Buzz stream are often bumped to the top of the list based on who last replied, so the more popular Buzz users tend to dominate the conversation. You can feed Twitter posts into Buzz to allow threaded comments on them, but Buzz posts do not feed back out into Twitter.

Figure 11–9. *Google Buzz*

Google's Buzz app for Android is a widget that allows for quick posts with photos, location information, and privacy settings. Reading Google Buzz is still handled through the mobile web browser interface, although this is something that will hopefully change with time.

Cross-Posting

So, once you're up and running with all these social media services, many of which use similar posting formats, how do you manage your time posting to them? You can take advantage of cross-posting tools and focus on the tool or format that is easiest or most rewarding for you. Increasingly, apps are offering built-in cross-posts to and from Twitter and Facebook.

If you're primarily a blogger but want to add tweets to announce new blog entries, one way to do it is through Twitterfeed, at `http://twitterfeed.com`. This is a free service that takes just about any blog feed and translates it into a shortened Twitter or Facebook post. You specify any prefix or suffix and how you want the post to be shortened, as shown in Figure 11–10.

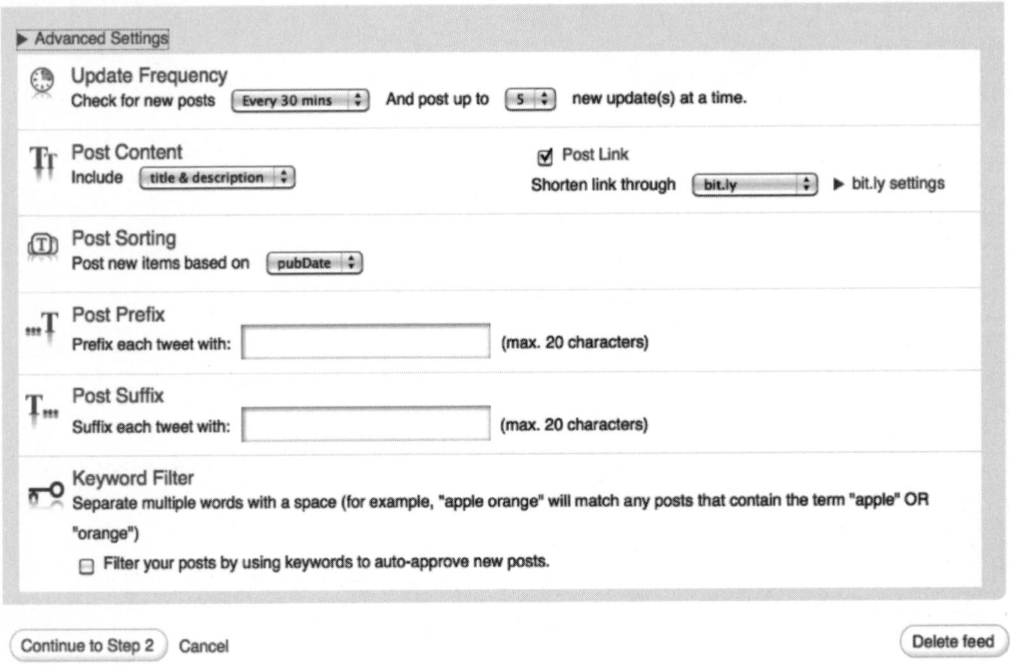

▶ Advanced Settings

🕐 **Update Frequency**
Check for new posts [Every 30 mins ⬍] And post up to [5 ⬍] new update(s) at a time.

T꜀ **Post Content**
Include [title & description ⬍]   ☑ Post Link
                                           Shorten link through [bit.ly ⬍] ▶ bit.ly settings

Ⓣ **Post Sorting**
Post new items based on [pubDate ⬍]

₊₊T **Post Prefix**
Prefix each tweet with: [   ] (max. 20 characters)

T₊₊ **Post Suffix**
Suffix each tweet with: [   ] (max. 20 characters)

⚷ **Keyword Filter**
Separate multiple words with a space (for example, "apple orange" will match any posts that contain the term "apple" OR "orange")
☐ Filter your posts by using keywords to auto-approve new posts.

(Continue to Step 2) Cancel   (Delete feed)

Figure 11–10. *Twitterfeed*

Networked Blogs (`www.networkedblogs.com`) is a tool for porting blog posts into Facebook fan pages. There are many other solutions as well, including free and paid apps.

If you want to go beyond simply scooping a feed from one place and putting it into another, you can use a more powerful cross-posting tool. Ping.fm, as mentioned earlier, is a free tool that can cross-post to Facebook fan pages. It can also cross-post to an impressive variety of social networks, blogs, and microblogs. From within Ping.fm, you can also make groups of media to post to; for instance, you could have a "press release" group that goes to your business Twitter account, Facebook fan page,

WordPress blog, and Delicious bookmark. Any post you make to that group is automatically cross-posted. AnyPost (Figure 11–11) is a fantastic free Android client for Ping.fm. You can use it to post to services one at a time or as a group.

Figure 11–11. *Ping.fm client AnyPost*

A similar tool for Android is Moby, though it is more blog oriented and does not post to as many services.

NOTE: As far as cross-posting is concerned, there's a fine line between posting the same message to multiple groups and simply spamming. The more places you cross-post, the more places you'll also have to monitor comments. Pay attention to how the big players in your market handle this balance.

Readers

If you want to read all your content in one place rather than posting it, you'll want an *aggregator* (aka *feed reader*). Feed readers take feeds from other sources and pile them into one place for easy reading. Tweets, blog posts, news items, and even Google searches are delivered as feeds that you can add to a feed reader, and many blogs add handy links for adding feeds. The universal symbol for an RSS feed is shown in Figure 11–12. When using most Android browsers and logged into your Google account, simply clicking the RSS icon in a blog will launch Google Reader and allow you to add the site's feed to your Google Reader account.

Figure 11–12. *Generic RSS Feed symbol*

Google Reader is a robust feed reader that lets you organize feeds by category, share likes, mark favorites, and leave comments. It also keeps track of where you read last. Unfortunately, official Google Reader support is currently only handled through the mobile web interface (shown in Figure 11–13), which is a capable app with a few shortcomings. The most important interface issue when using Google Reader through the web interface is that you can't use the Back button on your phone. It's a hard habit to break when you're used to navigating apps, but the Back button will exit your browser instead of going back to the previous feed.

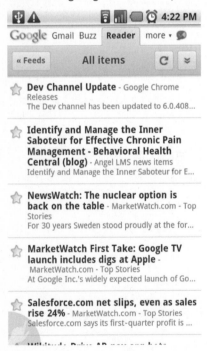

Figure 11–13. *Google Reader*

Some third-party apps support Google Reader, including free apps like NetaShare and paid apps like eSobi. You can specify whether you want feeds to sync in the background (if you're concerned about battery life, you do not) and how many feeds should be fetched at a time.

Summary

Social media encompasses a wide variety of tools and services. Just about everything posted, shared, or communicated online is done with a social purpose. This makes sense, because we are social creatures.

As social media has evolved, the media has begun to share with itself. Apps cross-post and share with each other, and aggregators read across many platforms. While you may not find an app with the sole purpose of posting to one blog or service, chances are that you can find one that posts to it among many. Use this power wisely. People like to be informed, but they do not like to be spammed.

CRM use of social media continues to evolve. One of the leaders in cloud-based CRM, Salesforce.com, announced it was releasing an Android app in late 2010. Salesforce's Chatter social platform will get an app in the first wave, and other Salesforce functionality will be added over time.

There's also a whole new class of social apps that were not discussed in this chapter. We'll get to location-sharing apps like Foursquare and Gowalla in the next chapter.

Chapter 12

Maps and Mobile

One of the big advantages of owning a smartphone is that not only do you have a mobile computer with you at all times, you also have a compass, map, and restaurant guide.

There is some variation in the hardware your phone has installed, but in general your phone can tell where you are by using the following:

- GPS (global positioning satellites)
- Cell phone towers
- WPS (Wireless Positioning System)

There are 27 global positioning satellites orbiting the Earth. Your phone's GPS unit attempts to find the signal from at least three of them and triangulate your position. However, this requires your phone to have a chip that detects GPS signals and be in an area that can detect them. If you're indoors or around lots of tall buildings, your phone might not pick up a GPS signal.

Your location can also be estimated using relative positions to cell phone towers. This isn't as accurate as GPS because cell towers are positioned for better signal reception, not triangulation, so there are generally not three overlapping points for positioning.

The third method of locating your phone comes from Skyhook Wireless and uses a map of known public Wi-Fi spots. Google uses a similar technique. It's a method that works well in urban areas and indoors—precisely the places where GPS does poorly. Because it only requires a Wi-Fi signal, it even works on laptops, netbooks, and tablets.

If you combine all three methods, you end up with a phone that usually knows where it is.

You can enable and disable your phone's ability to trace your location by pressing the physical Menu button while on the Home screen, and then Settings ➤ Location & Security. You can also install a Power Control widget (this comes standard on Nexus One) to easily turn your GPS on and off.

This chapter will discuss using Google Maps and other location-conscious apps on your phone for both business and pleasure. You'll learn how to use your phone for driving directions, deciding where to eat, and letting your friends know where to find you.

Understanding Google Maps

Most Android phones ship with Google Maps. It's optional and not part of the core Android apps from the Android SDK, but I've yet to see a phone that didn't include it. If you happen to have such a phone, it's a free download from http://m.google.com.

Google Maps works with your phone's GPS, and if you have location sensing enabled on your phone, Google Maps will determine your location when you launch the app. You can also use it to search for distant locations.

You can move your view of the map with your fingers, and in Android 2.1 and above, you can also use pinch-to-zoom motions to enlarge and shrink the area you're displaying. Android 2.0 and earlier users will have to use the zoom + and – buttons at the bottom of the screen, just as with a web browser. Click anywhere on the map, and Google will attempt to tell you the address of that location.

Press the Menu button to see your options, as shown in Figure 12–1. Remember that, if you're ever lost, you can use the My Location tool. You'll see yourself as a point on the map with a light-blue circle around it. Because there are a lot of variables that affect accuracy, the larger circle shows where you *could* be. The smaller the circle, the more accurate the prediction.

Figure 12–1. *Google Map options*

Driving Directions

If you just feel like exploring an area, use the Search button. You can either use the physical Menu button or the button that appears when you press the Menu button from the Home screen (as shown in Figure 12–1). This is useful for answering questions like "What's near 131st street?" or "Where is Uganda?" It's not, however, directions on how to get there.

In order to get actual driving directions, you should press Menu ➤ Directions. You'll see fields for My Location and "End point," as shown in Figure 12–2. The My Location field assumes that you want directions from your current location. If you want to use a different address, you'll need to enter it here.

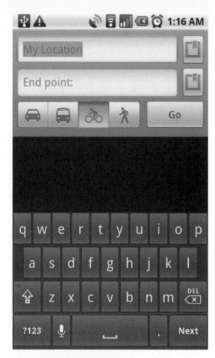

Figure 12–2. *Directions*

There's also a handy bookmark button right next to the My Location and "End point" fields. This lets you choose from your current location, a place you point to on the map, the address of one of your contacts, or any location you've starred. I'll cover how to add stars later in this chapter.

In Android 2.1 and above, you'll also see a series of buttons below these fields for choosing what mode of transportation you need. You can choose car, public transportation, bicycle, and walking directions. This is a lifesaver if you're trying to get anywhere in a big city without a car.

Once you've settled on a start point, endpoint, and means of transportation, click Go. You'll see a list of step-by-step directions in text. Click "Show on map" to see the route displayed on the map instead. If you leave your phone's GPS on, you can even see your progress as you go. I've used this to navigate New York City without annoying the locals by pausing too long to figure out directions.

Press the phone's Back button to get back to text directions. From here you can also press the phone's Menu button to get updated directions, reverse the directions for the trip back, or report a problem with the directions.

Map Layers

Google Maps for Android works by displaying information as a series of information layer overlays. If you're familiar with Google Earth, it works the same way. These layers can be turned on and off individually. Press the Menu button and then Layers to see some of the available layers, as shown in Figure 12–3. This list may also scroll. You can click the More Layers button to see even more layers. You can turn on more than one of these layers at a time.

Figure 12–3. *Google Map layers*

Traffic

Much of the information on Google Maps comes from contracts with third parties, and the traffic information is no exception. Traffic information is only available for large cities, and it's shown by color-coding the roads. Green indicates smooth traffic, yellow indicates delays, and red indicates major snarls. Traffic information can change rapidly, so don't expect absolute accuracy. It's also difficult (and dangerous) to check while you're actually on the road.

Satellite

Satellite info comes from a variety of third-party imagery sources, and those photos are stitched together and superimposed on the map information. Consequently, there are times when an address appears to be in the wrong location, and you'll notice patches of ground with different image quality.

Satellite images are also not immediate. The photos for any given area could be several years old. Google will often buy new images when something major happens in an area, such as Hurricane Katrina or the earthquake in Haiti, but don't be surprised if the satellite image of your house doesn't include your recently built garage.

Buzz

Google Buzz is a social networking tool (it was discussed in more detail in Chapter 11). You can make posts in Google Buzz that include your location information, and that adds your post to Buzz layer on Google Maps. Using this layer, you can see Buzz posts that were made nearby. The Google Buzz layer shows those posts as little quote bubbles over the map. Click a quote to see the post. Initially, this feature was only available for Android users with 2.0 and above phones, but now it is available for earlier versions of Android as well.

Google Labs Layers

Google Labs is shown in Figure 12–4. It is a collection of experimental features you can turn on and off. They're not always reliable, and they don't always last, but some Google Labs "graduates" have turned into solid and popular features, such as the public transportation directions in Google Maps.

Most main Google products have their own set of Google Labs experiments, and quite often (like in Gmail) those features just won't work on your phone. Google Maps is an exception.

To get to Google Labs, press the Menu button while in Google Maps, and then click More ➤ Labs. You can enable or disable layers at will. Google does use the relative popularity of Google Labs projects as one factor in determining what stays and what goes.

Figure 12–4. *Google Labs Layers*

Location Sharing with Latitude

Latitude is a way to let your social network know where you are. You can use it to make sure people know you made your flight, or let your contacts know you've got a trip in their city.

Currently, you can only share information with mutual friends, meaning you must invite your friends to share Latitude information with you, and they must accept the invitation. You can also use Latitude from a laptop or desktop computer, so it doesn't depend on everyone owning a phone. Your four global choices for sharing Latitude location information are

- *Detect automatically*: You just let your phone report where you are to your friends.

- *Set your location*: You can manually update your location (and lie about where you are if you wish).

- *Hide your location*: Nobody sees your location, but you can still see your friends.

- *Turn Latitude off*: You don't see where your friends are, either.

Keep in mind that your friends are the only ones who can see any of this, and settings for individuals will override global choices. Early after Latitude's release there was concern that someone could be stalked by having this feature turned on without their knowledge, so you may receive an e-mail letting you know you've joined Latitude or have turned on location tracking.

To add friends to Latitude from Google Maps, take the following steps:

1. Click Menu ➤ Join Latitude (Figure 12–1). Click Menu ➤ Add friends.

2. Choose to add through your contact list or by their e-mail address.

They'll receive an e-mail inviting them to join Latitude or accept your request. When someone sends you an invitation, you'll receive an e-mail asking if you'd like to ignore their request, share your location back, or accept their request and hide your location.

If all of this sounds a bit too personal, you can ratchet it down a notch for more casual business contacts.

To manage friends on an individual level, click Latitude and then click a contact's name.

You can see where they are on a map, contact them (via e-mail, Google Talk, etc.), get navigation directions to visit them, remove them as a friend, and set specific privacy settings. Click "Sharing options," and you can choose to do the following:

- Share the best available location (most likely your exact location)

- Share city information only

- Hide your information

You can change these settings later or tweak them by relationship level. Let your spouse know your exact location and your business contacts know your city only when you travel, for example. You can also globally shut them down by hiding, or manually enter just your city name when you don't need to broadcast your location.

Location Details

Do you need more information about a location? In the web version of Google Maps, Google has moved toward a system where each location has a *place page*. On Android, that means each location has a very well-organized detail page with tabs. Double-click a location or click the location bubble, and you'll see the location details, as shown in Figure 12–5.

Not every location will have so many details, so what you see will depend on the information available for the location. Also note that this is a fairly new feature, so sometimes the details themselves are off. In this case, reviews for Todd Rundgren are showing up for Google's Chicago office location.

Some details you can find include reviews, the location's web site, driving directions, distance from you, and the ability to share info about the location on social networks.

If there's an available phone number, you can call it by clicking the phone button.

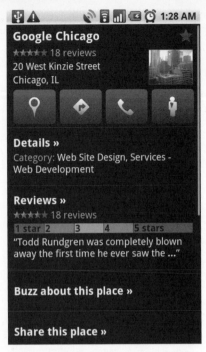

Figure 12–5. *Google Map location details*

> **NOTE:** If you need to give someone an address in a hurry, go to the location's details page, click "Share this place," and send it as an SMS text message. If they've got a smartphone, they can click the link you sent them and use Google Maps to get directions.

Starring Locations

You can also use the location details to add a star to a location. Click the star in the upper-right corner of the screen (shown in Figure 12–5). It will glow yellow when the location is starred. Simply click it again to remove the star. Using stars is like saving bookmarks for web pages. This enables you to easily find locations you visit frequently or need to find quickly.

You can access your list of starred items in Google Maps by going to Menu ➤ More ➤ "Starred items."

> **NOTE:** When you travel for business, put a star on the convention center and your hotel before you arrive, so you have instant access to the address, driving directions, the phone number, and nearby restaurants.

Google Street View

At first the idea seemed a bit creepy: Google used cars with mounted cameras and other equipment to take 360-degree photos of roads everywhere. It's still a bit creepy in light of their recent announcement that they may have inadvertently snooped on users in open Wi-Fi hotspots (this is another reason to use caution when using unencrypted hotspots).

That aside, Google Street View is an amazing tool for figuring out where you need to be. I use it when I have an appointment at a new location to see what the building looks like before I arrive, and check to see if there's any parking or tricky intersections along the way.

To get to Street View, go to the location details page (Figure 12–5), and then click the Street View button, which looks like a person with a triangle on their chest. Not every location has Street View, so if this button is grayed out, it's unavailable.

Navigate by dragging around the picture with your finger to pan around the scene. Go further up or down the road by clicking the arrows. The yellow line shows you the path the Street View car took as it traveled. Exit Street View with the Back button on your phone.

This process uses large pictures and takes some bandwidth, so you should only attempt it if you've got a fairly strong signal or are in a Wi-Fi hotspot.

Using Your Phone for GPS Navigation

If you have a phone with maps, wouldn't it be nice if you didn't also need a car GPS? As it happens, you can indeed use your phone as a GPS. If you don't have the latest version of Google Maps, you should download it from the Android Market to be sure you have Google Maps Navigation installed.

When you get driving directions, choose the Navigate option. This works best if you have a phone with a speaker phone option. Otherwise, you'll need to use a Bluetooth headset.

As you near your destination, Navigation will show you Street View, so you can glance (or better yet, have a passenger glance) to see where you're headed.

Many phones, like the DROID and Nexus One, have special car mounts for charging your phone while using it to navigate. The Nexus One mount defaults to using the Car Home app when the phone is docked.

Garmin introduced its own Android phone that offers Garmin's navigation software and a car mount accessory. It also includes Garmin Voice Studio to let you record your own voice for navigation directions. The big advantage of Garmin's phone is that the maps are downloaded and stored on the phone. This takes up significant storage space, but it means your phone is not dependent on a data connection for giving directions.

Car Home

Phones with Android 2.0 and above can use Car Home, a tool specifically made for using your phone in the car (Figure 12–6). Car Home assumes that you will mainly be using your phone for speaker phone-dialing your contacts and finding driving directions. In Froyo (Android 2.2), the Car Home app has also been redesigned to allow you to play music.

Figure 12–6. *Car Home in Android 2.1*

The buttons on Car Home are intentionally big, so you can press them with a glance instead of a stare. It works both vertically and horizontally, although it exhibits a few quirks in Android 2.1 that make it less than ideal as a true car navigation system. When someone calls you, you still have to drag to answer the call, and their contact info will be displayed horizontally.

Press the large microphone to launch voice search. You can use voice search to find a location. Unfortunately, in Android 2.1, it doesn't assume you also want navigation directions when you voice search, so you still have to do some hunting and poking. This means Car Home is really best used before you hit the road, or by a passenger.

If you don't like Car Home, you're not stuck using it for directions. Use the Navigation app instead.

Email and Text Directions

Other apps link to Google Maps, and Google provides plenty of alternative ways to find directions and locations. If someone sends you a location in Gmail, Google will sense that the information is an address, and attempt to automatically create a Google Maps link from it. Likewise, if you receive an SMS message with a Google Maps address link, you can use the link to launch Google Maps.

GOOG 411

One method of getting a business address from any phone in the United States is to dial (800) GOOG-411 (466-4411). This uses automated voice search by having you state the business name or category (like "pizza" or "flower shop") and the city and state.

Once Google finds your destination, you have several options. You can just listen to the address, you can say "text it" or "map it" and have Google send you an SMS message with the location, or you can have Google dial the business directly.

This may be an easier alternative in Car Home than trying to rely on voice search with no voice feedback.

Making Your Own Maps

You may have noticed that one of your options in Google Maps layers is "My maps." You're not limited to Google's layers in order to make a map. You can actually create your own map as a layer to Google Maps.

To create your own maps, you can either use Google Maps on a desktop computer, or you can download the My Maps Editor app from Google. This lets you add photos, lines, shapes, markers, and new addresses. Just click a location, click the + button (as shown in Figure 12–7), and select the type of content you want to add.

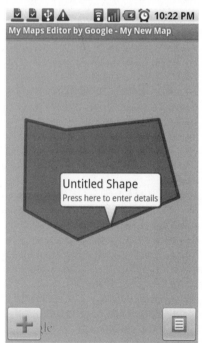

Figure 12–7. *My Maps Editor by Google*

Photos can only be added if you shoot them from your camera at that moment. Once you're done adding an element, you can add details to it. For instance, you could put a shape around the area of a convention where your company will locate their booth.

Once you've added the elements you need, click the Edit button and choose whether this is a personal, private, or public map, as shown in Figure 12–8. Give your map a name, and click the Save button.

Figure 12–8. *Saving a location in My Maps Editor*

All your maps will be available in the "My maps" layer, but only maps you've made public will be visible to other people or available in search.

Location-Sensing Social Media and Games

We've focused a lot in this chapter on Google Maps specifically. App developers are free to take advantage of the Google Maps library and Android's location-sensing features. There are countless restaurant-browsing and rating apps, many apps for finding specific services, and apps that tag photos or messages with your location.

However, one recent trend worth noting is location-sensitive social media. Latitude and Buzz use some of these features, and Twitter has enabled the ability to give location information, but two rising stars in this field are Gowalla (Figure 12–9) and Foursquare. Both were created around the same time and offer very similar features.

Figure 12–9. *Gowalla*

In both Gowalla and Foursquare, the object is to check into locations. You need to use a phone or other location-sensing mobile device. You can't just manually type in a location. You can share these check-ins with nobody, your friends, your Facebook page, or the whole world via Twitter.

Both Foursquare and Gowalla are working with businesses and cities to offer features like coupons and specials for users who check in. This unique form of advertising may become very popular, since you have an obvious way to measure the effectiveness of your advertising campaign.

Foursquare

Foursquare was cofounded by ex-Googler Dennis Crowley, who worked on a similar project, Dodgeball, which was purchased and abandoned by Google. However, Foursquare takes the social network to a new and different level by adding a gaming component. Dennis Crowley explained it to me as a method to combine exploring your city with gaming and a little bit of Boy Scout pride in earning merit badges and trophies.

Certain combinations of check-ins in Foursquare earn badges. Some examples include checking into the same location three times, finding five karaoke bars, finding three places in Chicago with photo booths, or checking in after 3 a.m. on a school night.

Checking into the same location regularly could also earn you a "mayorship." The mayor of a location is the person who has checked in the most often in the last two months, so you need to keep checking in to maintain the title. However, rapid checking in is disabled to avoid too many people gaming the system.

Gowalla

While Foursquare is a bit of a competitive game, Gowalla is more of a personal exploration and virtual geocaching tool. You can earn pins, similar to the badges in Foursquare, and you maintain a passport of places you've visited. You can also create and travel on tours of different check-in locations.

Gowalla also gives users a few virtual items they can leave or exchange at locations. Examples would be blankets, avocados, and espresso machines. When you encounter a virtual item at a location, you can see the history of who owned the item, encouraging the frequent exchange of these virtual geocaches.

Rapid check-ins are fine with Gowalla, since there's no mayorship. It's also much more sensitive to proximity than Foursquare, so you need to be pretty close to a location to check in. This makes it ideal for walking tours and pub crawls, but not great for check-ins within a building or anyplace where the GPS will not work well.

Summary

Location-sensing games are a growing trend, and social networks like Twitter and Facebook have started to incorporate the idea. Yelp, a social restaurant review site, has also added check-ins to its feature list. If your company is interested in location-sensitive promotions, it might be time to think about playing Foursquare or Gowalla to get a feel for the appeal.

Location-sensitive information also brings up privacy concerns. Pay attention to apps as you install them, and learn what they share and how to turn this sharing off when desired. New apps sometimes add features without thinking about the privacy implications, so just be aware that your location information may accidentally be tweeted or posted to Facebook. Generally, that's not a bad thing, but it doesn't look good if it happens when you're supposed to be at work, for example.

Android phones were built around location-sensing and maps. Using your phone, you can get walking directions, replace your car's GPS, and create and share a custom map. You can download custom apps that use map locations in ways that weren't possible before, such as bargain shopping, checking real estate values, and finding nearby movies. You can also share your location with friends in the hopes that you can see them in person more often.

Chapter 13

The Remaining Android Apps

I've covered the phone, e-mail, web browsing, and calendar. Now it's time to cover those remaining apps that are installed automatically on most phones and experimental Google features that could ship with future versions of Android. I'll discuss default Android 2.1 and 2.2 apps such as Search, the YouTube player, Music, the Clock, and the Calculator. I'll also discuss the power control, the News and Weather widget, Goggles, and gesture search.

I'll also discuss some of the options included with Android variations like HTC Sense and Motorola BLUR.

Calculator

One of the simple apps that ships with Android is a calculator, as shown in Figure 13–1. It has large buttons and does well with simple calculations. However, pressing the Menu button and then "Advanced panel" will bring up more advanced options like parentheses, trigonometry, and square roots.

If you need a true scientific calculator with graphs, you should download an app. There are a number of free apps capable of extending beyond the basic Calculator app, such as Scientific Calculator by Kreactive Technologies and Arity Calculator by Mihai Preda.

Figure 13–1. *Android Calculator*

Search

Search is what Google is known for, so it makes sense that search is a central part of Android. I've covered search in other chapters, so this is just a brief reminder that search is always an option. The Search widget comes preinstalled on most Android phones, and it includes voice search. In order to search, simply enter text in the text box. You can also use voice search, and this also works in versions of Android below 2.1 that do not support text-to-speech for other services. The Search widget will open a web session that searches Google for the intended word or phrase.

You can also search within individual applications by using the Search button. The main difference is that the Search widget will only search the Web, and the Search button will search your phone as well as the Web.

Gesture Search

As of Android 2.2, you still need to download this as a separate app for most phones. Some phones may include gesture software installed by the manufacturer. Samsung includes gesture search (Swype) in its modified Android phones, like the Behold.

Google Gesture Search (Figure 13–2) is an experimental search method that lets you draw letters on the screen with your finger in order to search your phone and the Web. It works best with large gestures forming uppercase block letters. As you write, search results from your apps and contacts will appear. As soon as you see your intended target, just click it.

Figure 13–2. *Google Gesture Search*

Goggles

Google Goggles (Figure 13–3) is an experimental app that attempts to search by phone picture. You take a picture of an item while using Goggles, and it will attempt to identify the item. If that fails, it will search for similar images. It works well for bar codes and terrible for plant or bug identification. Theoretically, you can also use it for identifying landmarks, books, DVDs, logos, and other items. You can also use it to translate text, which makes it handy for ordering from a foreign menu.

Figure 13–3. *Google Goggles*

I rarely find good results with objects or landmarks, but bar codes scan well. This highlights a problem with image search. It's very difficult and still in its infancy. As the technology improves, so will Goggles. For now, Goggles searches should be restricted to items that are consistent in shape and easy for machines to identify, rather than things like plants and animals that have a great deal of variation.

Alarm Clock

The alarm clock on Android (Figure 13–4) is powerful enough to allow you to ditch your standard alarm. Simply place your charger or charging dock near your bed. It encourages two good habits: getting up on time and charging your phone every night.

Figure 13–4. *Clock app when docked*

The Clock app automatically launches when Nexus One phones are placed in the dock accessory, and other phones may have similar accessories. It's also an alarm you don't have to turn off on weekends, because it will remember to let you sleep.

Launch the Clock app in Android 2.1 and above, and you'll notice that it lists the current time and weather. It also has four buttons on the bottom, as shown in Figure 13–4. One for alarms, one for slideshow photos, one for music, and a Home button for returning to the Home screen. The button at the upper right dims the contrast on the screen to let you get to sleep and keep the screen from being damaged. If you leave the Clock app running for a while, it will also automatically dim. Many versions also display weather information, so you know whether to wear your jacket as you leave for work.

Click the alarm button, and you'll see a list of possible alarm times, as shown in Figure 13–5. Alarms that are active have a green indicator light. Because you can have many different alarms, you can keep alarms you only need occasionally and only turn them on when needed. Need to get up an hour early? Just tap on the alarm once to activate it.

Figure 13–5. *Alarm times*

If you have an active alarm, no matter how far in the future, you'll see an alarm symbol in the notifications area at the top of the screen, as shown in Figure 13–5. When the alarm goes off, you'll have the choice of ending the alarm or snoozing it for a few minutes by pressing the appropriate button. If you are unfortunate enough to accidentally click the Home screen or Back button in a bleary-eyed morning haze, the alarm will still ring until you return to the Clock app to turn it off, unless you've set your side buttons to also dismiss the alarm.

Press the Menu button and then Settings while viewing your Alarms screen to fine-tune global alarm settings. The options in Android 2.1 and above include ringing the alarm even when your phone is set to silent mode, adjusting the volume of the alarm, setting the length of the snooze, and setting the behavior of the side buttons. You can allow these to do nothing, snooze the alarm, or dismiss it.

Powerful Alarm Options

Here's where it gets even more powerful. Click the alarm time (as opposed to the alarm clock symbol next to the time) to edit an alarm, or click the "Add alarm" button at the top of the page. You'll see the alarm details page (Figure 13–6). This offers a huge number of very practical options.

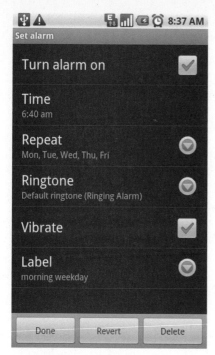

Figure 13–6. *Alarm details*

Setting the alarm time and turning it on are fairly obvious. You can also set the repeat. Choose "never" for an alarm you only use occasionally, but schedule your repeating alarms by the days of the week they repeat. Repeating alarms assume you need weekly scheduling, so you can't schedule an alarm to ring once a month. Figure 13–6 shows a work alarm that rings only on weekdays.

You can also pick the ringtone and whether or not this alarm vibrates. The default ringtone is a ringing alarm that resembles traditional alarm clocks with a shrill ringing bell. However, this is set individually per alarm. You could choose something quieter if your intent is not to wake up but to get something else done, such as getting out the door to get to work on time or picking your child up from theater rehearsals.

Finally, you can add a label to your alarm to remind you of its purpose. This label will show up in your list of alarms, making it even faster to turn the alarm on and off.

Analog Clock Widget

The Clock app in Android also comes with an Analog Clock widget. Unfortunately, you cannot change the style of the Clock widget in a standard version of Android. However, you can use the widget as a quick timepiece, and clicking it launches the Clock app.

Android variations, such as those found in HTC Sense UI phones, have much more elegant and beautiful clock widgets that combine the weather with the display. You can also download apps to improve the clock on most Android phones, such as the free Retro Clock widget, and the inexpensive **Beautiful Widgets**.

Some phones, such as the Android G1, ship with the Analog Clock widget already displaying. Simply long-click the widget and drag it to the trash to remove it.

YouTube

I discussed creating and uploading YouTube videos in Chapter 9. Now it's time to discuss browsing and viewing them. You can use your web browser to browse YouTube, and there is a mobile optimized version of the web site.

However, it is faster and easier to use Google's built-in YouTube app. Google provides a YouTube widget (Figure 13–7) you can install by long-clicking the Home screen. This widget is just a shortcut with three buttons. The YouTube logo launches the YouTube app. The magnifying glass launches search for the YouTube app, and the Camera button starts the camera to record videos.

Figure 13–7. *YouTube widget*

The YouTube app (Figure 13–8) is an easier, mobile-friendly way to navigate YouTube. Video thumbnail previews load last, so you can start browsing as soon as the app is launched.

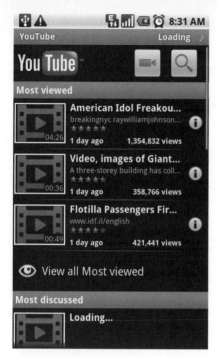

Figure 13–8. *YouTube app*

Logging into Your YouTube Account

You don't need to log into YouTube or have an account in order to view YouTube videos. You do need to be logged into an account to rate videos or view your subscriptions. From the YouTube app, press the Menu button, and then "My account." You'll be given a choice to use any valid YouTube account registered with your phone. If you still have a YouTube account that isn't linked to an e-mail address, you can use it as well by clicking "Add an account."

Browsing Videos

If you know what video you want to see, search for it by clicking the Search button at the top of the screen, or pressing the physical Search button on your phone. If you're not sure what you want to see, there are multiple ways to browse. Browse videos within the YouTube app by most viewed, top rated, and most discussed. When you're logged in, you can also view your subscriptions, your uploaded videos, and your "favorited" videos.

Ratings, Sharing, Comments, and Flags

Press on the "i" information button (shown in Figure 13–8) to get more information about a video. You'll see the rating, the date the video was uploaded, a description, the YouTube channel, and a list of related videos.

You'll also notice buttons to rate, view comments, add the video as a favorite, share the video, and flag the video as inappropriate/spam. Other than viewing comments and sharing the video, you must be logged in to use these options. Note that the comments button is a *view* comments button. You cannot make comments from the YouTube app at this time. This is speculation, but future versions of the YouTube app will likely allow you to make video comments from the front-facing camera on newer phones like the HTC EVO.

Playing Videos

Just click a thumbnail to start playing a video. Notice that the phone automatically displays videos in landscape mode no matter how your phone is oriented when you start playing them. You'll see video controllers to fast-forward, pause, or play the video. If you press the Menu button (as shown in Figure 13–9), you'll see sharing, comments, and other options. Pressing the "more" button will let you switch between low- and high-quality playback.

Sharing, as with most Android apps, will share the video with any app you have installed that supports sharing. With most users, this includes Facebook, Gmail, SMS messaging, and Google Talk.

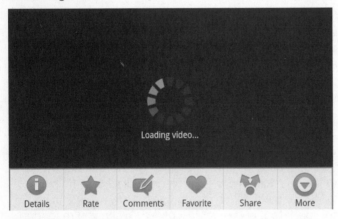

Figure 13–9. *Playing video*

Music

Android comes with a music player already installed (Figure 13–10). It scans your phone's SD card for music files and catalogs them for use. You can organize the files into subfolders for easier use. Supported formats include MP3, DRM-free iTunes M4A, Ogg Vorbis, AMR, and MIDI. These are all fairly standard formats that do not have DRM (digital rights management) software to restrict their use. That means some music you may have purchased for an iPod or other device will not work in Android.

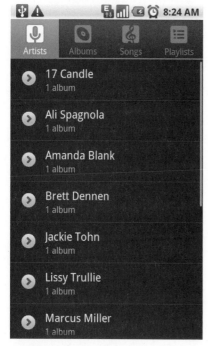

Figure 13–10. *The Music app*

The Music app also comes with a widget (Figure 13–7). The widget allows you to quickly launch playlists, pause or play music, and launch the Music app. Your phone may also have a docking accessory for playing your music on larger speakers.

Launch the Music app and you'll see music arranged by artist, album song, and playlist. To add to a playlist, long-click the name of the song, artist, or album, and choose "Add to playlist." You'll be prompted to either add to an existing playlist or create a new one.

> **TIP:** You can also use the Music app to turn your favorite song into a ringtone. Simply long-click a song (not an album or artist) and select "Use as phone ringtone."

News and Weather

Android 2.1 and 2.2 phones like the Nexus One come with a News and Weather app (Figure 13–11). This is a simple but elegant view of the current weather conditions and current events. Click it to view news and weather in more detail. Click any news headline to view all or part of the story.

Figure 13–11. *The News and Weather app*

Swipe your finger left and right to view tabs and categories, including the leftmost tab, weather. By default it's set to determine the weather from your current location, but if you wish you can monitor weather somewhere else. Press the Menu button while viewing weather, and then click Settings.

Drag your finger to the right to view news items. You're not restricted to the default choices here. If you don't care about sports and need to monitor news relevant to your occupation, it's easy to set it up. Press the Menu button and then click Settings ➤ News Settings ➤ "Select news topics." Check and uncheck boxes next to the news subjects you want displayed. Click "Custom topic" to add a custom search phrase for news.

When you use the News and Weather widget on your Home screen, headlines will appear from the topics you've selected for display.

HTC Sense

In earlier chapters, I talked about HTC and the Sense UI. When you use a phone with Sense, as shown in Figure 13–12, you'll notice that the bottom portion of the phone does not have the usual app tray. Instead, it has a central phone button to launch the Dialer app and a small contact button on the right. The left has a small arrow button to open the app tray.

Figure 13–12. *HTC Sense UI Home screen showing enhanced widgets (image courtesy of HTC)*

Most of Sense UI's features are implemented through widgets. However, there is a very convenient interface tweak for navigating between pages on the Home screen known as Leap. You can swipe your fingers just as with other phones, but you can also make a pinching motion on the screen. This brings up a thumbnail preview of all the Home screen pages. Just pinch and then touch a thumbnail to navigate to that screen directly. Leap is only available on more recent Sense phones.

HTC's widgets offer attractive calendars, social networking integration, and creative clock/weather displays. Friend Stream (Figure 13–13) is a Sense social network aggregation tool that pools Twitter, Facebook, and other social networking updates, so you can track updates without having to check separate services.

Figure 13–13. *Friend Stream on an HTC Legend (image courtesy of HTC)*

MOTOBLUR

Motorola MOTOBLUR uses a similar social aggregation approach for phones like the DEXT (but not the DROID). It includes both the Messages and Happenings widgets, and apps for cross-network status, photo, and e-mail tracking. MOTOBLUR also allows you to integrate Exchange and Google Calendar in a single display. Android 2.2 supports Exchange calendar integration.

Summary

Android ships with a surprising amount of apps to turn your phone into a mobile communication, news, and music entertainment center. The Clock app allows you to have both a travel and bedside alarm clock that remembers when you need to get up early and when you want to sleep in.

Many phone carriers offer preinstalled apps for their customers. Sometimes these apps are carrier exclusives, and sometimes they are merely preinstalled for convenience. T-Mobile offers Sherpa on some phones, an app for locating restaurants and entertainment destinations near you. It also offers My T-Mobile, an app that tells you your current plan and your current phone minute and text usage.

Sprint and AT&T offer entertainment channels. Verizon offers Skype Mobile on most Android phones. The Garmin Garminphone offers a built-in Garmin GPS. As Android releases stabilize, expect more offerings from carriers to differentiate themselves from the competition.

Chapter 14

The Android Market

The Android Market is the primary place for downloading apps for your Android phone. Some phones also ship with access to device-specific app stores as well, but all of the phones so far can use the Android Market. Some devices, like the Android-based Nook, are not intended for use with the Android Market.

Right now, there are several versions of Android shipping on phones you can buy new. So how do you know if your Android 1.5 device will run the latest Twitter app? The general rule is that, if you can see it, you can run it. Developers can exclude incompatible devices from seeing their apps in the Android Market.

In this chapter I'll go into more detail about how you download and find apps, how you leave feedback, and how you can try before you buy. You'll also learn about eleven must-have apps to download right now.

QR Codes

Before we go further, let me introduce you to QR (quick response) codes (Figure 14–1). You may have seen these square bar codes on objects or web sites. The QR Code was patented by the Japanese company Denso Wave. Rather than restrict use with licensing fees, Denso Wave chose to allow anyone to generate or use QR codes without having to pay a fee, and their use has been growing as smartphone use grows.

Figure 14–1. *Example QR code (goes to the XZing Barcode Scanner app)*

QR codes can contain all sorts of information, like map locations, URLs, notes, names, phone numbers, and product identification. You don't have to worry about scanning them right-side up; upside down and sideways will work, too. They're easily read by phone cameras, so they make an ideal way to offer information to phone users without requiring a lot of typing. In fact, you may want to print a QR code on the back of your next business card, so smartphone users can scan in your contact information immediately. You can generate your own codes from `http://zxing.appspot.com/generator`.

Your phone may not have shipped with a bar code reader. There are countless apps in the Android Market that allow you to scan QR codes, including Google Goggles and ZXing's Barcode Scanner.

In this chapter and beyond, I'll use QR codes whenever possible. If you're reading this book with an Android phone in hand (and not reading this book *on* your Android phone), just use the QR code to get to your app faster.

Browsing the Android Market

You can visit the Android Market Showcase on the Web at www.android.com/market, although this site will only show you a fraction of the available apps. You'll need to use your phone to see the apps available for your specific phone model and version of Android. Launch the Android Market app from your phone's application tray or desktop. The initial page will look similar to Figure 14–2, with buttons for apps, games, and downloads; a splash banner; and a list of featured apps.

> **NOTE:** You can also browse available apps on the Web at www.androlib.com and www.androidzoom.com. These are both ad-sponsored sites that pull data from the Android Market, but as third-party sites, they don't always have the most complete listings.

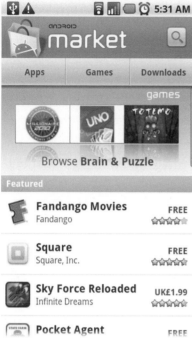

Figure 14–2. *Android Market*

Notice that each app lists a rating out of five stars, as well as its price. You can click an app to read more details about the app, including user reviews. Sometimes you may want to browse through the featured apps to see what is new. Sometimes you know exactly what you want, and sometimes you want to browse, but only within a category, such as productivity apps or shopping. The Android Market gives you the choice. Some phones have a carrier button instead of a Downloads button. Verizon DROID users will see a Verizon button, and G1 users will see a T-Mobile button, for example.

If you're feeling precise, use the Search button at the top of the screen. You can search for a name or keywords. For instance, searching for "Twitter" would show you both the official Twitter app and apps that use Twitter in their description, such as HootSuite.

Navigating by Category

To navigate by category, click the Apps button and then select a category. You'll see three new buttons at the top: "Top paid," "Top free," and "Just in" (Figure 14–3). By default, the "Top paid" category is selected, but you can switch to free or recent apps by clicking the appropriate button. Apps are weighted by popularity, not strictly listed by rating. This is because it's easy for an app to get a five-star rating if only one person has rated it.

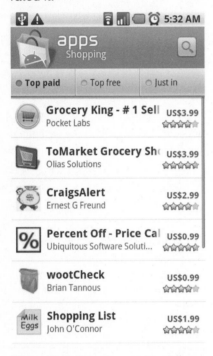

Figure 14–3. *Browsing apps by category*

Click the name of an app to see the details page associated with that app. You'll see the name, rating, two screen captures, the price, and a description of the app submitted by the developer. You'll also see any web site and contact information the developer has provided, such as an e-mail address and phone number.

If you scroll down the page (Figure 14–4), you'll see any user-submitted comments. The last three comments are shown, but you can click the "Read all comments" link to see more. You'll also see information about the developer, and links to any other apps they may have developed. If the app is deceptive or malicious, the very bottom of the page gives you room to flag it.

You may notice that each comment has a box with an *X* in it under the rating. Use this box to flag any spam comments you may see. Press the box, and you'll see a confirmation message asking if you want to flag the comment as spam. As soon as you confirm, the offending comment will disappear from your screen.

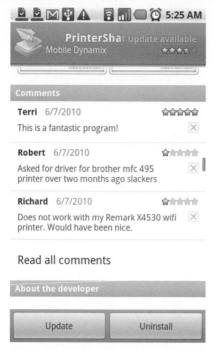

Figure 14–4. *App details: comments*

Comment Differences in Android 2.2

In Android 2.2, there are a few changes to the Android Market to make the experience of browsing and evaluating apps more intuitive. Rather than being at the bottom of the page, comments have their own button, as shown in Figure 14–5. Rather than just an *X* to delete spam comments, you see an up or down arrow for rating the comments. You can rate comments as helpful, unhelpful, and spam. This is similar to the way users can rate Amazon.com reviews.

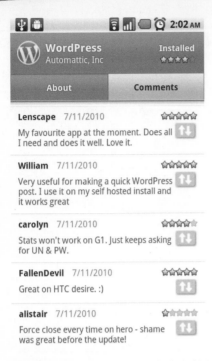

Figure 14–5. *Rating comments in Android 2.2*

Paying for Apps

The Android Market has a huge selection of free apps, but there are times when it's worth it to buy an app. You can use Google Checkout or direct phone carrier billing, where available. Currently, T-Mobile is the only supported carrier for direct billing (and for US dollar transactions only), but as Android gains momentum, this is sure to change.

Google Checkout is an online payment-processing system. Register for a Google Checkout account by going to http://checkout.google.com and using the same Google account you use as the main account for your phone. You can enter your credit card information and Google will store it. Register in advance to avoid the hassle of entering credit card info on a phone keyboard.

You can purchase apps in most foreign currencies using Google Checkout and your credit card (Figure 14–6). Google will give you an estimate of what the price is in US dollars. However, your credit card may charge you a fee for currency conversion or use a different exchange rate, and that won't be reflected on the bill.

Figure 14–6. *Processing a payment in a foreign currency*

NOTE: You have 24 hours after purchasing an app to "return" it for a full refund.

Downloading Apps

Other than payment processing, the basic steps to downloading an app are the same. Go to the Android Market, navigate to the details page, and click the Install button at the bottom of the screen. Android will confirm that you want to download the app, and it will also show you specific information (Figure 14–7) about what the app has permission to do with your phone. In most cases, the uses are quite legitimate, but you should read them carefully to make sure a word puzzle game doesn't have access to dial your phone, for example.

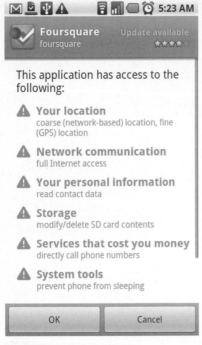

Figure 14–7. *App permissions*

If everything looks good, click the OK button. Your download will start, and you'll see a progress bar in the Android Market and notice in your notification bar that a download is in progress. The notice will change once the download is complete. There's no need to keep using the Android Market app while you're downloading. The download will continue in the background.

Installing Apps

In most cases, downloading the app installs it automatically. If there are any widgets included with the app, you'll need to long-click the Home screen to install them. If there are additional steps, the developer should provide instructions. In the case of some paid apps, you may have two downloads. The first is a trial version, and the second is a separate key that doesn't actually do anything other than unlock the full features from the first app.

> **NOTE:** Android 2.2 (Froyo) allows developers to give you the option to install apps on your SD card instead of the phone's hard disk. This can potentially save some space. However, it is up to the developer to allow the option in their app.

Uninstalling Apps

There are two basic ways to uninstall an app. The more complicated method is to go to the Home screen, press the Menu button, and then click Applications ➤ "Manage applications." Click the app you want to remove, and then click Uninstall.

The second, much easier method is to find your app in the Android Market, navigate to the detail page for that app, and click the Uninstall button. If you paid for the app, you'll see an "Uninstall & refund" button, as shown in Figure 14–8. You have 24 hours after a purchase to return it for a refund. However, you must do this through the Android Market.

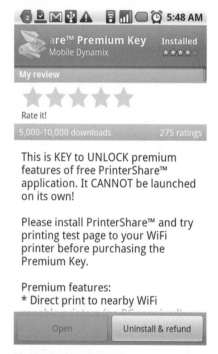

Figure 14–8. *Uninstalling*

You'll see a warning window telling you that you're about to uninstall an app. You'll also be told whether or not you can install the app again at no charge. In the case of paid apps, not only must you pay for it again (since you're being refunded), you cannot return it twice for a refund.

Android also collects data on why you chose to uninstall an app. Select a reason or "I'd rather not say," and then OK.

Updating Apps

Occasionally developers will add features or bug fixes. When there's an update available, you'll see an alert in your notification bar at the top of your Home screen. You can click the alert to go directly to the Android Market, or you can launch the Android Market app and click the Downloads button (Figure 14–9). If you don't see a Downloads button on your phone, press the Menu button to reveal it.

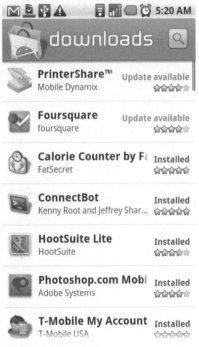

Figure 14–9. *Updating*

Click an app to view the details, and then click the Update button at the bottom of the screen. The process is very similar to downloading an app. In Android 2.1 and earlier, you must do this individually for each app, but in Android 2.2 you can update everything at once by clicking "Update all." For apps that you'll unhesitatingly update, you can also specify that you'll allow automatic updates on that app's About page in the Android Market. Checking that box means available updates will automatically install as soon as they're available. Even if you choose automatic updates, you'll have to manually install app upgrades that change an app's permissions.

CAUTION: Read the comments before updating an app or allowing automatic updates. Sometimes the update will break something or not work with particular phone models.

Rating and Commenting

If you've installed an app, you may want to go back and tell other users how well it works. Even a comment verifying that it works on your model of phone is helpful. The first step is to rate the app. The ratings area is at the top of the app's detail page under the section "My review." Click the stars, and you'll see a rating screen resembling Figure 14–10. Indicate the number of stars the app deserves by dragging your finger left to right. Once you are finished, click OK.

Figure 14–10. *Rating an app*

Once you've rated an app, you'll see a link to post a comment right under your rating. You can only comment on apps you've rated.

Installing Apps Outside the Android Market

In most cases, the Android Market is all you need to find apps for your phone. However, developers aren't required to offer their apps through the market. App developers in countries that don't yet support paid apps through the Android Market may want to sell paid versions of their apps outside the market, for example. This also allows developers to create alternative app markets, like SlideME (http://slideme.org). You can download apps from other locations, but you need to enable downloads from unknown sources to authorize it. To do so, from the Home screen, press the Menu button, click Applications, and then toggle the box next to "Unknown sources" (Figure 14–11).

Figure 14–11. *Installing from unknown sources*

Now you can download apps that aren't in the Android Market. If you know the location of an app, you can navigate there through your phone's web browser and install it. Android apps have the .apk extension. Download the APK file, and then click the message that the download is complete in your notification bar. You'll see a screen asking you if you'd like to install the app (Figure 14–12).

Keep in mind that this isn't a move without risks. Apps could have been removed from the Android market for malicious activity, and those apps can be remotely removed from your phone when you install them using the Android Market. You can still see the permissions required by the app, so be mindful before you install.

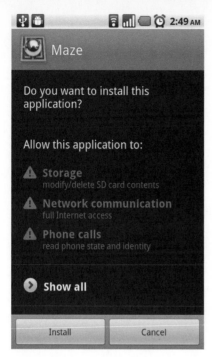

Figure 14–12. *Installing APK files*

Eleven Must-Have Apps

If you asked me tomorrow which apps I must have on my phone, I'd give you a different answer than I will today. There are a lot of quality apps available, so here are a few of my favorite general-use apps. I've provided the QR code, so if you have a bar code-scanning app already installed, you can scan in the code and navigate to the Android Market directly.

ShopSavvy

ShopSavvy is a longtime favorite free app (Figure 14–13). It debuted on the Android and really showed off the potential of the phone. It uses your camera to scan in bar codes and comparison shop with both local and online items. Local shopping results are sometimes limited.

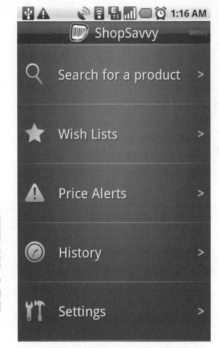

Figure 14–13. *ShopSavvy*

You can set price alerts, tweet about your scans (although this gets obnoxious), view your history, create a wish list, and more. If you're searching for an item that either doesn't have a bar code or has a store sticker over the bar code, you can also enter your search terms by hand.

Best of all, ShopSavvy supports QR codes, so if you download this app first, you can scan any of the QR codes you see in the rest of the book.

Lookout Mobile

Lookout Mobile (Figure 14–14) is a free app that provides three valuable services: phone location, virus protection, and backup. You can enable or disable the services as you choose. For remote location and backup, you need to register with their web site at www.mylookoutmobile.com. You can also schedule backup times for times when you know your phone will be in its charger.

Virus protection may not seem like a huge deal right now, but as smartphones and the Android platform gain popularity, it's a problem that could grow. Lookout Mobile scans apps as you download them, which means downloads do take slightly longer to install.

Figure 14–14. *Lookout Mobile*

Mint.com

Mint.com is Intuit's free, online personal finance software. The official Mint.com app (Figure 14–15) is also free and gives you access to your personal finances, including a widget. You can choose whether the phone remembers your data or requires a password each time you log in. Just make the appropriate choices in the app's Settings menu by pressing the Menu button.

Remember, if you choose to install the Mint.com widget portion, you're exposing your financial data to anyone within eyesight.

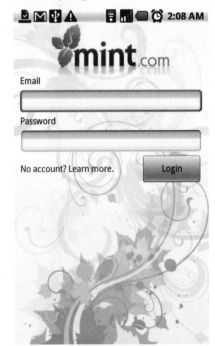

Figure 14–15. *Mint.com*

Cooking Capsules Taster

Cooking Capsules is an innovative approach to selling recipes. The Taster module (Figure 14–16) is free, but the Brunch app is a premium app. However, at $0.99, it's not going to break the bank. The app offers you brief video instructions on preparation, a shopping list you can check off as you purchase, and then a checklist of cooking instructions based on the video you've already seen.

Even if you're not much for cooking, the app itself is a great example of how-to content that takes advantage of mobile features.

Figure 14–16. *Cooking Capsules Taster*

Evernote

Evernote is a web service at www.evernote.com that allows you to keep virtual scrapbooks of notes, pictures, web clippings, and audio files. You can add tags and search terms to your notes and access them anywhere on the Web. This means you can make a grocery list and have it available on your phone. Take a picture of something on the road and examine it from your desktop computer. Take a quick audio note or picture in the parking garage to remember where you parked.

The Evernote app (see Figure 14–17) is free, and the basic Evernote service is free. Evernote also offers a premium subscription service with higher storage limits.

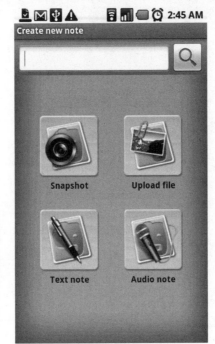

Figure 14–17. *Evernote*

Pandora

Pandora is an Internet radio service that lets you create custom "radio stations" based around a song or group (see Figure 4-18). The playlist won't consist entirely of songs from that band, but they will share common style features as analyzed by the Music Genome Project. You can refine the choices with a Like/Dislike button. It's a great way to find new music you didn't realize you liked, and it's a great way to listen to music on your phone without having to download it.

Figure 14–18. *Pandora radio*

Pandora offers free (ad-sponsored) listening for 40 hours per month. You can upgrade to a premium account for $36 a year with unlimited listening and no ads. The Android app is free either way, but subject to the same limits of the user's account.

Toddler Lock

If you have a child that likes to play with your Android 1.6 and earlier phone, Toddler Lock (shown in Figure 14–19) is a must-have. It locks the phone buttons but tells you the unlock combination in text. Dragging fingers along the phone's surface draws random, colorful shapes and lines while a tinkling music plays. Obviously, there's some potential for your child to smash the phone to pieces, but there are often occasions when having a small, brief distraction comes in handy.

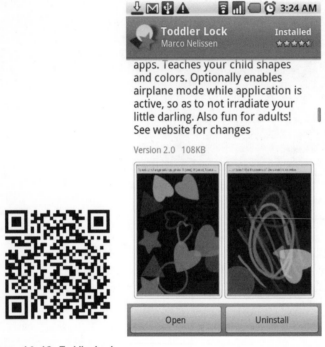

Figure 14–19. *Toddler Lock*

Android 2.1 and 2.2 users should consider the toddler app AnimalFun instead.

New York Times

The official New York Times app (shown in Figure 14–20) is a free app that lets you see the newspaper's content in a format optimized for mobile viewing. It's also easier to carry around than a full paper. There's no registration required, and at this point there appears to be no advertising for anything other than home delivery of the Times. That may change in the future, so enjoy the free app while you can.

Figure 14–20. *New York Times*

Google Voice

I've mentioned Google Voice in earlier chapters, so I won't go into a lot of detail. If you've registered for Google Voice, the app (shown in Figure 14–21), which includes the ability to quietly check your voicemail messages during a meeting, is definitely a must-have.

Figure 14–21. *Google Voice (image courtesy of Google)*

WikiMobile Encyclopedia (Bonfire)

It may not be the most accurate encyclopedia, but it's certainly a great first start. If you find yourself looking things up in Wikipedia all the time, it makes sense to have an app that can do that for you. WikiMobile Encyclopedia (see Figure 14–22) uses less bandwidth than your web browser, so you get the results faster. Swipe through pages one at a time. There's also a back/forward option for navigating densely linked pages.

Figure 14–22. *WikiMobile Encyclopedia*

Yelp

There are countless restaurant-finding apps for phones these days, but Yelp (see Figure 14–23) has a vibrant user community and ratings for just about every location. Find a restaurant, bank, gas station, or drugstore near you, at home, or on the road. The straightforward interface and copious reviews make this a must-have for anyone who travels or just likes to eat out.

Figure 14–23. *Yelp*

Summary

The Android Market offers an elegant solution for app downloads, both paid and free. Although critics had doubts that users would like using Google Checkout for payments, the system works well and even offers a money-back guarantee.

I'll get into more details when I discuss advanced troubleshooting, but you need not worry about losing all your paid apps if your phone should ever crash. Just go to the Android Market and click the Downloads tab. There's a record of your downloads and the fact that you paid for them. The information is stored on the Web, so it isn't wiped clean if your phone needs to be reset. Simply click the links and download your apps again.

Chapter 15

General Business Applications

I've discussed the basics of navigating your phone and using the built-in apps. I've also talked about installing and buying apps and using QR codes. Now let's get to work. Here are some of the best apps for general office and business use. Some of them were mentioned earlier in the book. In this chapter, I'll also include a QR code for easy downloading. If you scan the code and can't find the app in the store, it most likely means it's not available for your phone or version of Android.

Document Tools

If you work in an office, chances are you need to deal with documents. In Chapter 8, I discussed Android's capabilities to interact with Microsoft products. At the time of this publication, there are no solutions to reading OneNote on Android. That may come in the future, but for now, I'd recommend using Evernote instead.

Of the document management software I tested, DataViz Docs to Go (Figure 15–1) was the stablest and offered the best interface for both viewing and editing documents. However, you may have different results with different phones, so the best approach is to use free trial versions and compare against the types of documents you'll typically use. Docs to Go allows some editing and formatting, and it will even handle DOCX files. It's not a replacement for a full-sized word processor, but it is a good complement to one.

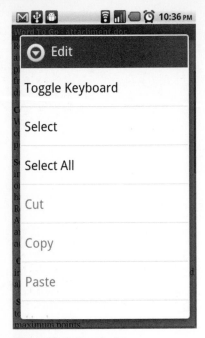

Figure 15–1. *Docs to Go*

ThinkFree Mobile is another popular choice, though in my testing it suffered from more formatting errors when trying to display documents. Table 15–1 shows these and more document tools.

Table 15–1. *Document Tools*

App Name	Price	Notes	QR Code
Docs to Go, by DataViz	Free trial/$14.99	The free trial allows you to view, and the paid version allows you to edit. It supports Word and Excel formats. The paid version also supports PowerPoint.	
OfficeSuite Viewer, by Mobile Systems	Free trial/$1.99	The free trial is a 30-day trial. The app supports Word, Excel, PowerPoint, and PDF files. This had a high failure rate in my testing when trying to open files.	

App Name	Price	Notes	QR Code
ThinkFree Office Mobile, by ThinkFree Mobile	Free/$9.99	The free version is just a viewer. The paid version can be purchased either item by item (word processing, spreadsheets, slide show), or all at once. It will download and open Google Docs, and has a built-in file browser. Overall, this is a nice feature set, but in my testing it did not display documents well and often made them difficult to read with black backgrounds.	
Adobe Reader, by Adobe	Free	Allows you to view PDF attachments but not create or edit them. This is stable, free, and offered directly from Adobe. It also supports pinch-to-zoom and viewing from the Web.	

Printing

If you've got a document ready for printing, why not print it directly from your phone? PrinterShare (Figure 15–2) lets you do exactly that. However, it doesn't yet support printing Word and Excel files, so this is most useful for printing photos, not office documents. You also need to install desktop software in order to print to non-Wi-Fi printers. The free trial lets you print a test page to verify that it will work.

Figure 15–2. *PrinterShare*

As Android gains popularity, expect to see more printing solutions, but at the time of this publication, it's a lonely field. Table 15–2 shows PrinterShare, the only app in this category.

Table 15–2. *Printing*

App Name	Price	Notes	QR Code
PrinterShare Droid Print, by Mobile Dynamix	Free trial/$4.95	Use the free trial and test-print before committing to a purchase. Be aware that Office files are not supported, but PDF and photos are.	

File Management

Not only is it nice to be able to view or edit your document attachments, but it's nice to be able to know where those files are stored on your SD card without having to connect your phone to a computer in order to do basic file management tasks.

File management lets you see and move your files, which also means that you can break things if you don't know what you're doing. Use caution when moving files and renaming folders. Of the apps I've evaluated, EStrongs File Explorer (Figure 15–3) was my personal favorite, but there are many strong, free choices.

Figure 15–3. *EStrongs File Explorer*

I like to combine this with Dropbox, which allows me to share and sync files through the Internet and access them from any computer or mobile device. Table 15–3 shows file management options.

Table 15–3. *File Management*

App Name	Price	Notes	QR Code
EStrongs File Explorer, by EStrongs	Free	This app allows copying, moving, multiple selections, ZIP expansion, app management, FTP (File Transfer Protocol), and Bluetooth file transfer.	
AndExplorer, by LYSESOFT	Free	This app allows copying, moving, GZIP, and other file management functions with a straightforward user interface.	
File Manager, by Apollo Software	Free	This app has a cleaner interface than EStrongs, but does not include Bluetooth transfer.	
Linda File Manager, by Nylinda.com	Free	Linda File Manager is also a solid choice, but also lacks Bluetooth support.	
Dropbox, by Dropbox	Free	This app allows Dropbox users to access and share files between users and computers as if they share a common folder. Basic accounts are free, and premium accounts offer more storage. Visit the web site at www.dropbox.com for more info.	

Virus Protection, Backups, and Security

Viruses may seem like a remote worry, but as mobile use becomes more popular, people will figure out better ways to distribute them. However, losing your phone or having it stolen are big potential problems right now, especially if you store sensitive data on your phone. It may be a job requirement that you be able to wipe business data from your phone if it is stolen.

Some phones ship with remote wipe and location already installed, and Android 2.2 allows remote wiping of Exchange data.

As discussed in Chapter 14, Lookout Mobile (Figure 15–4) is my personal top pick in this category, but I do not have a remote wiping requirement. It's free and provides three services within one app. If you feel the virus protection is unnecessary, you can also disable that portion and just use the other two services. I also appreciate that it sends you an e-mail whenever you use remote location to make sure your online account hasn't been breached.

Figure 15–4. *Lookout Mobile*

Free remote location apps set Android apart from the iPhone, where remote location requires a subscription to a .mac account. Table 15–4 shows virus protection and other security options.

Table 15–4. *Virus Protection, Backups, and Security*

App Name	Price	Notes	QR Code
Lookout Mobile Security Free, by Lookout	Free	This app provides virus scans, remote location, and file backup. The remote location can either show you where your phone is on a map (if GPS is enabled) or emit a loud alarm.	
KeePassDroid, by Brian Pellin	Free	This is a password manager based on the open source KeePass project. You can combine this with Dropbox to make a cloud-based password safe.	
WaveSecure, by WaveSecure	$19 per year	WaveSecure offers theft protection with remote location, remote lock, and remote wiping of the data on the SD card.	
Norton Security Beta, by NortonMobile	Free trial	This is a beta release with an unknown pricing model for the full release. The features include virus scanning, call screening, remote wipe, and remote lock.	
Super Private Conversation, by Superdroid.net	Free	This app blocks unwanted SMS and phone calls and filters specified SMS conversations for privacy.	

Presentation Software

Most of the document management software listed earlier can handle viewing PowerPoint files. Chances are slim that you'll need to actually present *from* your Android phone, but, if you need to, you can use Docs to Go or the slideshow feature in your phone gallery in a pinch.

At this time, most Android phones do not support TV out, so you can't just plug it into a TV or monitor and see video images. This is a hardware—not software—limitation, so most of us actually giving presentations using Android phones are stuck projecting them from an Elmo. However, the Droid Incredible and HTC EVO *do* come with TV out capabilities, which means future phones may do the same. That also means you can pair them with portable projectors that take standard TV connections, use MightyMeeting (Figure 15–5), and leave the PC behind.

Figure 15–5. *MightyMeeting*

Don't have a phone with TV out? There are still plenty of other ways Android can help your presentation. Table 15–5 shows some of your options.

Table 15–5. *Presentation Software*

App Name	Price	Notes	QR Code
MightyMeeting, by MightyMeeting	Free	This app allows PowerPoint and Keynote presentations from the phone. It can be used to either lead or attend live conferences with invited attendees. Files must be uploaded to your MightyMeeting account first in order to be available as presentations. More information is available at www.mightymeeting.com.	
Oration Sensation, by EpiCache	Free	Oration Sensation is a presentation timer that offers vibrating timed alerts at preset intervals. You can save a list of presentation types, such as "short sales pitch" or "conference presentation," and keep your phone in your pocket. The alerts will let you know when it's time to switch slides or move to Q&A.	
Remote for PowerPoint, by Johan Brodin	Free	This lets you use your phone as a Bluetooth remote for PowerPoint presentations. Test it beforehand (obviously), because not all computer and device combinations will be compatible.	
Gmote 2.0, by Marc Stogaltis and Mimi Sun	Free/$2.99	Gmote is a general Wi-Fi remote control for your PC that can be used for music files as well as PowerPoint. It's cross-platform compatible, so you can use this to control Mac media as well. However, it requires server software to be installed on the computer you want to control, making it a no-no for some work environments. The $2.99 version is "donateware" for the developers.	

Web Conferencing

At this time, the only Android phone that allows true video conferencing is the HTC EVO, so there isn't a lot of mobile software for video conferencing. However, Web conferencing from your phone is starting to emerge as a real possibility. WebEx and GoToMeeting don't have official apps at the time of this publication, but that may change as their competitors eliminate the need for a PC. As mentioned earlier, MightyMeeting offers the ability to host and attend live conferences without requiring a laptop client. Table 15–6 shows some handy apps for web conferencers.

Table 15–6. *Web Conferencing*

App Name	Price	Notes	QR Code
MightyMeeting, by MightyMeeting	Free	This app uses www.mightymeeting.com. If you own a phone with TV-out capability, you can present directly from your phone to the screen. You can also use this for live meetings with live chat feeds from users on a variety of phone platforms or using the Web. (Currently, mobile attendees must have US phone numbers.)	
Fuze Meeting, by FuzeBox	See note	Fuze Meeting is a subscription Web conferencing service. The Android app is free, but the presenter must have an account with Fuze Meeting. More information is available at www.fuzemeeting.com.	
Vibrate During Meetings, by Sidetop Software	$2.99	This doesn't create Web conferences. It just makes you more polite during conferences and other scheduled meetings. When your calendar says you have a meeting, your phone will switch to vibrate.	

Note Taking

It's doubtful you'll want to take traditional notes during a meeting from your phone, but you may want to access notes you've taken earlier or leave yourself quick sticky notes. Some apps are also tied into to-do lists. Evernote is one of my favorites, and it was listed as one of my must-have software picks in Chapter 14. I enjoy the ability to take a voice or picture note.

You may prefer mind mapping to traditional note taking. Android can help with that, too. Thinking Space (Figure 15–6) is one of several mind mapping applications that allow you to diagram words and ideas visually rather than creating bullet point lists.

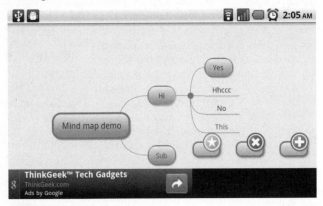

Figure 15–6. *Thinking Space*

Table 15–7 shows Thinking Space and other note-taking options for Android.

Table 15–7. *Note Taking*

App Name	Price	Notes	QR Code
ColorNote Notepad Notes, by Notes	Free	This is a virtual sticky note app for your phone. Take quick, color-coded notes or make simple to-do lists.	
Notebook, by Darkgreener	Free/£.99 (about $1.55)	This note-taking app uses an old-fashioned book font for a more formal feel, but it also has some nice features. The full version allows e-mail import and password protection.	
Mind Map Memo, by Takahicorp	Free/¥180 (about $2.08)	This is a simple mind mapping app. The paid version provides a few additional features like extra node options.	
Thinking Space, by Charlie Chilton	Free	Thinking Space is a full-featured mind mapping tool that offers a lot of customization options.	

E-mail Management

I discussed e-mail in an earlier chapter. Android has very capable native options for e-mail, but in the corporate world you may need more than what comes in the Android box. If your device is running Android 2.2 and beyond, you may not have as much of a pressing need for a separate Exchange e-mail app, but TouchDown (Figure 15–7) will still be very helpful if you do. It's also an option if you want to keep a strict wall between your work and private e-mail and calendar space, since TouchDown's calendar does not sync with Google Calendar.

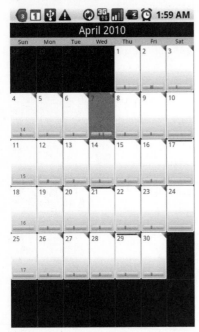

Figure 15–7. *TouchDown*

Table 15–8 shows some e-mail management apps.

Table 15–8. *E-mail Management*

App Name	Price	Notes	QR Code
Exchange by TouchDown, by NitroDesk	Free trial/$19.95	Also see "Exchange for Android" for Android 2.0 and 2.1 devices. TouchDown supports security policies and ActiveSync. You can also specify times to turn off push notifications. TouchDown also comes with a variety of widgets. It does not merge your Gmail and Exchange calendars or tasks. After the trial expires, you can still use some but not all features.	
RoadSync 2.0, by DataViz	Free trial/$9.95	This offers similar features to TouchDown. After the trial expires, the product is disabled.	
Gmail Speech Alert Trial, by Webcipe	Free/$2.99	This is a text-to-speech app for your Gmail messages. It also supports Bluetooth, but it does not currently support Android 2.2.	
SpamDrain, by SpamDrain	$30 per year	SpamDrain is a web-based spam-filtering service. All filtered messages are still available via the web site, and messages not marked as spam are delivered to your inbox. The app comes with a 30-day trial.	

To-Do Lists

You can use a widget bookmark for Google Tasks, but it's easier and more efficient to use a dedicated app. Google didn't write it, but gTasks ToDo (Figure 15–8) syncs with Google and gives it Android app power with an easier user interface. If you use the Pure Calendar widget, you can display gTasks to-do items as part of the widget.

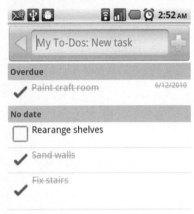

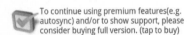

Figure 15–8. *gTasks to-do list*

Table 15–9 shows gTasks and other to-do apps.

Table 15–9. *To-Do Lists*

App Name	Price	Notes	QR Code
gTasks ToDo for Android, by SSI	Free	Provides online and offline Google Task syncing. This feels like the missing app Google should have created. There is a paid version of the app that includes autosyncing, but it is not sold through the Android Market.	
Astrid Task/Todo List, by Todoroo	Free	Astrid is an open source task management tool that syncs with Remember the Milk. It's a solid choice for anyone that doesn't need Google Task syncing.	
Got To Do Lite, by Slamjibe Software	Free/£2.00 (about $3.14)	This app is based on the "Getting Things Done" system (created by David Allen).	

Expenses and Finance

I hate tracking expenses, but it's a necessary evil. I was very happy to learn about web-based services like Expensify and Mint.com (Figure 15–9) that would handle most of the data entry for me and let me just see the results.

For personal finances, Mint is my favorite. You must have a Mint.com account to use the app, but it keeps easy track of your accounts, portfolio, and budget, and sends you e-mail or text alerts for events you specify, such as when you are charged a banking fee, when you make a large purchase, and when your bills are due.

Figure 15–9. *Mint*

Table 15–10 shows some of my favorite finance apps.

Table 15–10. *Expenses and Finance*

App Name	Price	Notes	QR Code
Mint.com Personal Finance, by Intuit	Free	You must have a Mint.com account. Both the service and the app are free. Mint.com makes its money through sponsored offers for credit cards and other financial services.	
Expensify Expense Reports, by Expensify	Free trial/$4.95	Expensify is a web-based service for creating expense reports "that don't suck." Most transactions come directly from your credit card as you charge them, but this app is used for entering cash transactions and taking photos of other receipts that are not automatically entered. More information is available at www.expensify.com.	
Personal Assistant, by Pageonce	Free/$7.00	Personal Assistant combines bank and credit card management with travel itineraries, frequent flyer mileage, phone minutes, Netflix, and portfolio management.	
Finance, by Google	Free	This is Google's official app for Google Finance. It offers multiple-portfolio support and stock quotes.	

Travel

If you have to travel for work, you'll appreciate travel apps that track your mileage, give you your schedule (Figure 15–10), help you find places to eat, and make sure you don't say anything embarrassing to the locals. Google Maps comes with the default Android installation and includes public transportation directions when available, but there are third-party apps for specific cities available, so don't forget to search the market before you travel. Google Maps for Android also includes the Places icon, which allows you to browse nearby locations by category.

Figure 15–10. *TripIt*

My favorite travel app, aside from the preinstalled Google Maps, is TripIt (Figure 15–10). It allows you to see your itinerary and share it with close contacts while providing general information to professional contacts or the public in general. TripIt can also be tied in with LinkedIn and Facebook.

Table 15–11 shows TripIt and some other travel app options.

Table 15–11. *Travel*

App Name	Price	Notes	QR Code
TripIt Travel Organizer, by TripIt	Free	TripIt is a web-based service that tracks your travel itinerary and mileage. The phone app gives you your flight schedule and appointment information on your phone.	
Topo Maps Lite, by Trailbehind	Free/$3.99	This app provides offline road and topographic maps for times when you're traveling out of cell tower range. It's aimed at outdoor sports, but it's still very useful for traveling to rural areas.	
Geodelic, by Geodelic Systems	Free	This is also known as Sherpa on some phones. Geodelic finds nearby restaurants, cafes, attractions, and so on. You can browse by category of food or distance.	
Google Translate, by Google	Free	This is Google's official app for Google Translate. Not only does it translate text to and from over 50 languages, it also has an audio pronunciation guide.	

Summary

Android offers a surprising amount of very useful apps for general business use, and the amount of offerings is growing at a phenomenal pace. There's a fantastic selection to make travel, task management, communication, and presentation easier. In the next chapter, we'll look at some more specialized apps for professionals.

Chapter 16

Specialized Apps for Professionals

In the previous chapter, we looked at general business applications. In this chapter, we'll look at more advanced apps and apps for more specialized fields of work. Are you a doctor, lawyer, firefighter, or real estate agent? There are apps for you.

As with the last chapter, you can use a bar code-scanning application to navigate directly to the app in the Android Market, and if you can't find the app, chances are that it doesn't run on your particular phone.

Health and Medicine

Health care professionals were among the first to see the immediate usefulness of mobile technology, and app writers haven't ignored this. Epocrates has a long tradition of offering its reference materials on PDAs and other mobile devices, and pharmaceutical companies such as Novaris are making their own apps.

Medical Spanish Audio was my favorite app of this group. It lists Spanish phrases by category, such as trauma assessments (Figure 16–1). If you check the box next to a question, you can bookmark it for reference, and if you click a question, the app will pronounce it out loud for you.

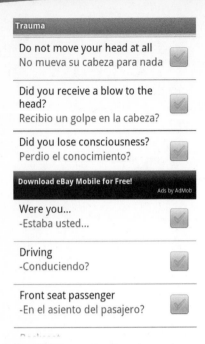

Figure 16–1. *Medical Spanish Audio*

See Table 16–1 for more health and medicine apps.

Table 16–1. *Health and Medicine Apps*

App Name	Price	Notes	QR Code
Epocrates Rx, by Epocrates	Free	Epocrates Rx is a free reference app for drug information. As of this publication, the software is still in beta, so Epocrates may choose to charge for a premium service or full version in the future.	
Skyscape Medical Resources, by Skyscape	Free	This is a general medical reference, including prescription and over-the-counter medicine.	

App Name	Price	Notes	QR Code
Medical Spanish Audio Lite, by Mavro	Free/$6.99	This is an app for non-Spanish-speaking care providers to use to communicate with Spanish-speaking patients. The paid version removes the ads.	
Medical Mnemonics, by Regular Rate and Rhythm Software	$1.99	Not a medical professional . . . yet? This app helps students study with a library of mnemonics and the ability to create and submit your own.	

Law and Legal

For those working in or around law offices, there are reference materials and news sources. DroidLaw (Figure 16–2) is a good example of this. You can use it to sort through legal procedures, but it also can track many popular legal blogs and news feeds.

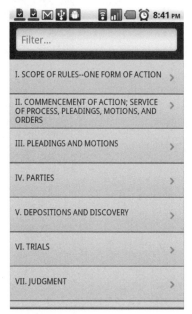

Figure 16–2. *DroidLaw*

For legal students, there are lots of study guides and flash card games. There are also a few specialized apps for calculating billing hours and target dates. You may also consider apps like Locale that automatically turn your phone's ringer off at certain locations, such as the courthouse. See Table 16–2 for example law and legal apps.

Table 16–2. *Law and Legal Apps*

App Name	Price	Notes	QR Code
DroidLaw, by BigTwit Software	Free/varies	DroidLaw is a legal reference app. The base app is free, but you can expand it through paid apps with the material you need, such as Supreme Court cases ($2.99) or United States Code ($3.99).	
LangLearner Legal Dictionary, by LangLearner	Free	This app is a simple dictionary of legal terms for lawyers, legal assistants, and people studying law.	
Wathen Legal News, by Genwi	Free	This app provides international legal news stories and allows you to comment.	
Lawyer's Calendar Calc, by Hawkmoon Software	Free/$1.99	This app calculates target dates and numbers of workdays between two dates for legal billing purposes.	

Real Estate

Real estate agents can also benefit from many more generalized apps, such as to-do lists, galleries, e-mail apps, and note-taking apps. There are also a number of apps using the MLS database both for professionals and consumers. Zillow (Figure 16–3), for example, is a Google Maps-based app that makes estimates of house values and shows current listings. If you click a property listing, it will show a picture of the property and details. It provides useful general information for both consumers and agents.

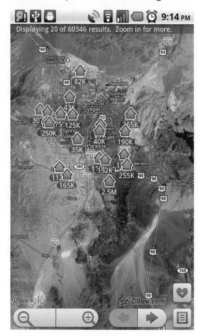

Figure 16–3. *Zillow*

See Table 16–3 for more real estate apps.

Table 16–3. *Real Estate Apps*

App Name	Price	Notes	QR Code
Mortgage Calculator, by Adonis Apps	Free/$4.99	This is a fairly straightforward mortgage and autopayment estimator with PMI (private mortgage insurance). It relies on data from Bankrate.com. The pro version offers more options.	
Mortgage Pro, by Skynet Creations	Free	This is a mortgage calculator that helps buyers evaluate 15- or 30-year mortgages, points, balloon payments, and other mortgage options.	
RE/Max University, by Mediafly	Free	This app was written specifically for RE/Max agents and includes corporate communications and training videos.	
Real Estate Vocabulary Quiz, by Upward Mobility	$2.99	Studying for a real estate broker exam? This app offers vocabulary quizzes. The company also offers many state-specific versions.	
Zillow Real Estate, by Zillow	Free	This app comes from the same makers as the Zillow web site. This gives estimates ("Zestimates") of property value and shows listings on a map.	

Sales and CRM

CRM (customer relationship management) seems like something that was meant to be done from your phone. You can find tools that work with Microsoft CRM, and Salesforce.com is developing tools that are not yet on the market. There are plenty of smaller CRM companies that are willing to work with Android, such as Simply Sales (Figure 16–4), and several developers have introduced standalone apps for the freelancer.

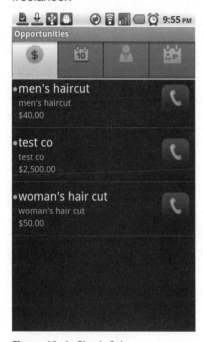

Figure 16–4. *Simply Sales*

If you're interested in using CRM apps, try a few out to see what works for you. See Table 16–4 for sales and CRM apps.

Table 16–4. *Sales and CRM Apps*

App Name	Price	Notes	QR Code
Locale, by two forty four a.m.	$9.99	Locale sets your phone's ringer behavior based on the time, who is calling, what is on your schedule, and the phone's location. Set it to stop ringing during sales meetings or prioritize some calls over others. Many other apps also work with Locale's settings.	
Mobile CRM for MSCRM, by Softtrends Software Private Ltd	Free trial/$99.00	This app is a third-party solution for connecting to Microsoft CRM. The full version is expensive, so take advantage of the fully functional trial to see if it will work.	
Simply Sales, by MyOlive.net Small Business Portal	Free	Simply Sales is a simple CRM app that integrates with Gmail and Google Maps. The app was written by MyOlive.net, which also offers a small business CRM portal.	

Retail

Small business retailers will really appreciate being able to accept and process credit cards from their phones. For the most part, these apps are free; however, you must have a merchant account, and they charge membership and/or transaction fees for credit card processing.

FaceCash (Figure 16–5) also promises an innovative way to let retailers and merchants handle transactions. Rather than carrying a credit card, FaceCash allows users to show merchants an ID that prominently showcases a picture of their face and transfers the funds from an account with FaceCash rather than a credit card. Users can choose to tie their bank account to the payment service or rely on transfers from other customers (such as parents). Think PayPal with an easier ID system. However, FaceCash isn't useful if nobody accepts it and nobody asks to use it, so most merchants will still need to process credit cards.

Figure 16–5. *FaceCash*

See Table 16–5 for a selection of money-processing retail apps.

Table 16–5. *Retail Sales Apps*

App Name	Price	Notes	QR Code
Pocket Verifier, by MerchantAnywhere	Free app/$299 hardware	More information is available at www.merchantanywhere.com. This app uses your phone's Bluetooth to process credit cards from a device sold separately. It only runs on Android 2.1 and higher.	
Mobile Credit Card Processing, by Merchant Swipe	Free	This app will work on early phones like the G1. However, it requires you to manually input the credit card information on the phone rather than giving you a swipe reader. More information is available at www.merchantswipe.com.	

App Name	Price	Notes	QR Code
Square, by Square	Free	Square is a relatively new company that's been making a splash with its payment system. Square has promised to send a free credit card reader to merchants signing up for the service, but several comments in the ratings indicate that this may not be happening in a timely manner.	
FaceCash, by Think Computer Corporation	Free	FaceCash is a way for purchasers to use their phone for payments instead of carrying their credit card. They use the app for payment. It shows the merchant a picture of the true phone owner's face for security verification, and no paper or plastic needs to change hands. Both the purchaser and retailer must have accounts.	

Finance

Android lends itself to personal finance and portfolio management software. One example is Google's own Google Finance app (Figure 16–6). Google Finance allows you to track general stock direction, portfolios, and financial news.

There are also many apps written specifically by banks for their customers. Always double-check the author and reviews when downloading an app that claims to have been written by your bank.

Figure 16–6. *Google Finance*

You'll also find currency converters, MBA study guides, and basic expense management software. See Table 16–6 for a few apps that stand out either by offering more features or superior look and feel.

Table 16–6. *Finance Apps*

App Name	Price	Notes	QR Code
Google Finance, by Google	Free	This is the official Google Finance app; it includes stock quotes and finance news.	
Personal Assistant, by Pageonce	Free/$7.00	Personal Assistant combines investment portfolio and personal bill management with flight itineraries, cell phone minutes, and monitoring your Netflix queue.	
pFinance, by BiShiNews	Free	This app is a personal finance manager that also tracks portfolios and financial news. What makes this app so nice are the simple calculators in the Finance column. They include things like a tip calculator, an interest calculator, and a currency converter.	

Project Management

Project managers have to keep track of a lot of parts and people in order to do their jobs. It seems ideal to be able to do some of that tracking from a mobile device, rather than having to lug around a laptop or transfer handwritten notes.

Mobile Project Manager (Figure 16–7) is very capable for a mobile app. It can import from MS Project format, create Gantt charts, and send reports via e-mail. You can add both location and contact resources, and attach files from your phone's SD card.

Figure 16–7. *Mobile Project Manager*

Mobile Project Manager does have an overexuberant help screen that tries to pop up every time you enter a file, but you can uncheck the box set to display the help screen at all times in order to remove this annoyance.

See Table 16–7 for project management apps.

Table 16–7. *Project Management Apps*

App Name	Price	Notes	QR Code
Upvise Pro, by Unyverse	Free trial	This app handles simple CRM and project management.	
Mobile Project Manager, by Hawkmoon Software	Free/$2.99	This is a simple project manager that allows import and export of Excel files and sharing.	
Time Tracker, by Sean E Russell	Free	This is a simple time-tracking app for figuring out time spent and generating reports on projects and tasks.	

Education and Training

Higher education institutions have begun offering apps aimed at students, including maps, enrollment information, and access to the campus learning management system. Both Blackboard and Moodle developers have recognized that students may want to access coursework with a mobile phone. In Moodle's case, they've worked on optimizing the mobile browser experience for general usability on all mobile platforms without a dedicated app. Blackboard is partnering with Sprint to offer the option of a free native app for Sprint customers. Schools that wish to support other phone networks pay an additional licensing fee.

Currently, most Android apps aimed at students focus on eBooks, flash cards, grammar, and study guides. There are some true gems among these apps. Google Sky Map (Figure 16–8) shows a view of the stars that changes as you change the angle you hold your phone (as if your phone has become a virtual telescope). Likewise, Google Earth provides a virtual globe with layers of customizable information about the planet.

Figure 16–8. *Google Sky Map*

Table 16–8 shows some education apps for both teachers and students.

Table 16–8. *Education and Training Apps*

App Name	Price	Notes	QR Code
Grade Rubric, by Android for Academics	Free/$0.99	This is a simple grading app for teachers that use rubrics. The paid version can e-mail final grades. It does not tie into a learning management system at this time. The company is developing a version that will sync with Google Docs and create a grade spreadsheet.	
Google Sky Map, by Google	Free	This app shows a map of the stars, but that is a simple explanation. It's one of the apps I regularly pull out when people ask why they'd want a smartphone.	
Blackboard Mobile, by Blackboard	Free	This app only works with institutions that are running Blackboard's learning management software with the mobile plug-in. It allows students to participate in distance-learning courses from their phone.	
Formula Droid, by Abhishek Kumar	€1.50 (about $1.95)	This is a scientific calculator and formula reference guide for students; it includes things like periodic tables and a web reference.	
PlinkArt, by Plink Search	Free	Reference materials aren't limited to calculators and star charts. PlinkArt is a reference tool for artwork. It also has a scan and identify feature using your phone's camera to try to identify art, but, as with Google Goggles, this isn't completely reliable. Visual scanning is still too new, but it may be a conversation builder to guess what elements are causing PlinkArt to guess incorrectly.	

Social Media

Social media has become an important part of doing business, as our social lives move to the Web and word-of-mouth is replaced by viral marketing. I already discussed social media and Android in Chapter 11, but I can't emphasize enough how mobile these social networks have become. Figure 16–9 shows blog posts made using the WordPress app for Android. I doubt anyone will use the app to write novels on their phone's virtual keyboard, but using this app makes it simple to take a photo from your phone and quickly blog about it.

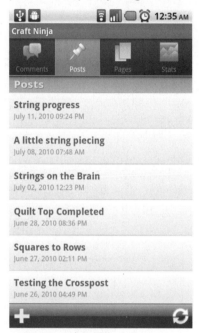

Figure 16–9. *WordPress*

Table 16–9 describes a few of the apps mentioned in Chapter 11 to get you started using social features on your phone.

Table 16–9. *Social Media Apps*

App Name	Price	Notes	QR Code
HootSuite, by HootSuite	Free/$2.99	HootSuite is my top pick for Twitter on Android. Schedule tweets, manage multiple accounts, and see analytics. The paid version offers more features.	
WordPress, by Automattic, Inc.	Free	If you have a WordPress blog, whether on WordPress.com or on your own server, this app will let you post to it (provided that your blog is WordPress 2.7 or higher and has the correct server settings enabled).	
Google Buzz, by Google	Free	This simple widget allows quick posts with pictures and/or location information to Google Buzz.	

Information Technology

Your IT staff may have already installed, modified, and mastered these apps for Android, but if you're looking into using an Android phone, it's good to know you can manage your server or answer help desk tickets from your phone. Not only are there a wide variety of IT tools for Android, a large portion of them are free and written for the convenience of IT professionals, such as the difficult-to-read but very useful ConnectBot (shown in Figure 16–10), which allows for SSH (Secure Shell) connections from your phone.

Figure 16–10. *ConnectBot*

Table 16–10 lists a few such apps that don't require special phone hacks to work.

Table 16–10. *IT Apps*

App Name	Price	Notes	QR Code
Zendesk for Android, by Zendesk	Free	This app is for existing Zendesk customers. It allows you to remotely track and manage help desk tickets.	
android-vnc-viewer, by androidVNC team + antlersoft	Free	This is a simple, open source VNC (virtual native client) viewer for Android. It connects to TightVNC, RealVNC, and Apple Remote Desktop.	
ConnectBot, by Kenny Root and Jeffrey Sharkey	Free	ConnectBot is a simple, open source SSH client for Android. It's difficult to see the tiny text, but it makes up for this by giving you the ability to copy and paste.	
IPConfig, by Mankind	Free	This is a simple utility to tell you statistics about your current Wi-Fi connection, including your IP address and DHCP server.	
AndFTP, by LYSESOFT	Free	AndFTP is an FTP and SFTP (Secure FTP) app for Android. It also allows open, rename, cut, paste, delete, and other basic functions. Although I doubt you'd want to use this to set up and configure web sites regularly, it works well for fixing small problems quickly.	

Other Apps

Here are a couple of apps that are worth mentioning, even if they don't quite fit into one of the broader categories. Although it may belong in education app category, until Amazon adds better audio navigation for the user interface, the Kindle likely will not replace the textbook on campuses. However, for the mobile professional, eBooks are starting to come of age. Amazon chose an eBook format incompatible with industry standard ePub books, but made up for it by developing apps for most mobile platforms, including Android, as shown in Figure 16–11.

Figure 16–11. *Kindle for Android*

The user interface for Kindle for Android is more intuitive than the standalone Kindle eReader because you can swipe your finger to turn pages rather than pressing a button. You also don't get a month-long battery life on your phone, but the books are still easy to read, even on a small screen.

Firehouse Scheduler is another great app, created for emergency responders. It is designed to keep track of shift schedules.

If you or your business owns a car, aCar is a great app to use to make sure you take care of it. Table 16–11 lists both of these apps, along with Kindle for Android.

Table 16–11. *Other Apps*

App Name	Price	Notes	QR Code
Kindle for Android, by Amazon	Free	Purchase, download, and read Kindle books from your phone. The app keeps track of your downloads and reading progress between devices, so you can start a book on an iPod and finish reading on your Android phone.	
Firehouse Scheduler, by Leaky Nozzle	$5.99	This app is an emergency responder's scheduler. It's designed to track shifts, vacation time, paydays, sick time, and traded shifts. Leaky Nozzle also has a variation specific to the New York Fire Department.	
aCar, by Armond Avanes	Free	This app tracks car expenses, maintenance, and mileage. It has reminders for regular maintenance items like oil changes. Whether you're maintaining a business or personal car, this app is useful.	

Summary

The Android Market is still very young, but it is already seeing tremendous growth. As I am writing this, there are over 76,000 apps available according to Androlib.com, a web site for browsing Android apps. By the time this book hits publication, there will likely be well over 100,000 apps. That's still not as many as there are available for the iPhone, but considering there were only 50,000 apps available a month ago, it's likely Android will soon surpass Apple in app availability.

Because Android has an open market system that doesn't charge developers an annual fee or require a lengthy approval process, there's room for app developers to fill niche markets and create highly specialized apps. That's good news for professionals. Keep an eye on the Android Market for new apps.

Chapter 17

Advanced Customization and Troubleshooting

In this chapter, we'll look at ways to go beyond standard Android use and customization. We'll look at modifying the phone with themes and how to measure widgets. We'll also look at how to troubleshoot some common problems, reboot your phone, and upgrade Android. We'll also look at what it means to "root" your phone, including the pros and cons of doing so.

Advanced Widgets

When you add widgets to the Home screen, most widgets are already a predetermined size and shape. Either they fit in the space given or they do not. If you long-click a widget, you can move it within a screen, but you cannot make it larger or smaller. If you have a choice of widgets, you'll find that many app developers label the widgets with things like "3×2" or "4×1."

What does that mean? If you measure your phone's screen not by the physical screen size, but by the number of apps you can store on it, most phones have a Home screen that measures four app icons by four app icons. The widget measurement generally goes horizontally by vertically, so a widget that measures 4×1, such as the Power Control widget (shown at the top of the screen in Figure 17–1), takes up the space of four apps across and one down. This allows you better Home screen space management.

Figure 17–1. *Widget size*

Themes

If you want to give your phone a complete makeover, you can use one of many Home replacement themes. Most themes at this time are written for Android 1.5 and 1.6, and are designed to run using a specialized app that acts as a theme engine. They replace your standard Home screen and sometimes modify the appearance of the icons used to launch your apps. You could turn all of your icons into spaceships, sports icons, or cartoon figures with a matching background.

Popular theme engines include Freshface (shown in Figure 17–2) for G1 and MyTouch phones, aHome, Open Home, and Panda Home. The disadvantage of running a Home replacement theme is that it is essentially running an app all the time. That means it may drain your battery faster or make your phone crash more often. Be sure to check out the comments in the Android Market before downloading a new theme.

Figure 17–2. *Freshface theme*

Skinnable Widgets

Rather than using a Home replacement app, you can often just use a combination of widgets and background images to change the appearance of your phone. Some widgets even allow you to modify their appearance with themes you can download separately. The Weather & Toggle widget ($1.99) offers so many skinning options that it becomes difficult to find the base app in the Android Market. Figure 17–3 shows the QR code.

Figure 17–3. *Weather & Toggle widget*

Live Wallpapers

Android 2.1 and above introduced the "live wallpaper." This is a background wallpaper that can be animated and react to events on your phone, like touching the phone, the time of day, or the sounds playing on your phone. Several live wallpapers come with Android 2.1, but you can also download new wallpapers both as free and paid apps. Figure 17–4 shows the Shake Them All! Live wallpaper by Yougli, which includes the Android logo falling in slow-motion on your screen, and reacting to shaking and being touched.

Figure 17–4. *Live wallpaper*

The disadvantage of live wallpapers is that they take more power to display, especially if they have interactive features. Just like everything else, they're also a small program running in the background, so if you find your phone crashing more often, try switching to a different wallpaper.

G1 users can't use live wallpapers, but they can visit G1Wallz.com for wallpapers specifically designed for the G1. Wallpapers can also be installed straight from your Android phone's web browser. Some wallpapers may not be appropriate for the workplace, so browse from work at your own risk.

Managing Battery-Draining Activities

Live wallpapers, data use, GPS, and apps that constantly update in the background can drain your phone's battery pretty rapidly. If you notice that you're not getting the battery life you'd hoped for, you can check to see where the blame lies as follows:

1. From the Home screen, press the Menu button.

2. Select Settings, and then scroll to the bottom of the screen. Click "About phone."

3. Select "Battery use."

You'll see something resembling Figure 17–5. This shows you what has used the most batteries since you last unplugged the phone. Apps are listed, as well as system functions. It's not abnormal to see an app or activity using more battery power once in a while, but if you notice a pattern, it's time to change your behavior or delete the offending app.

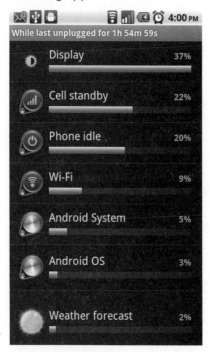

Figure 17–5. *Battery use*

If you want more specific info about an app, you can press the name of the app on the screen. You'll see a detail screen (Figure 17–6) showing more specific info that also gives the amount of phone CPU power the app uses and the amount of data it has sent and received. Some apps (in Android 2.2) may also allow you to adjust the power usage.

Figure 17–6. *Battery use details*

Clicking the "Application info" button shows yet a third layer of information about that app (see Figure 17–7). From here you can force an app to stop running, uninstall it, and see specifically which permissions that app has. You can also clear data on an app, but do this with caution. That means you'll have to re-create any settings or data you've entered before.

Some of what you'll see depends on which version of Android you're using. Android 2.2 (Froyo) supports storing apps on the SD card. This is only an option if it's specifically allowed by the programmer, which is why the option is grayed out in Figure 17–7.

Figure 17–7. *Application info*

Also remember that your network use can affect your power. Android phones can use 2G, 3G, and in some cases 4G networks. The rule of thumb is that the faster the signal, the more it will drain your battery. One notable exception is Wi-Fi, which will generally not drain your battery as fast as 3G access, though there's no point in leaving Wi-Fi on when you're out of Wi-Fi signal range.

Over-the-Air Updates

Over-the-air (OTA) updates are firmware updates for your phone sent by your carrier. Updates come to some phones and carriers earlier than others. While you can check to see if any updates are available, you can't induce an OTA update to happen any faster.

To check to see if your phone has any updates, take the following steps:

1. From your Home screen, press the Menu button, and then click Settings ➤ "About phone."

2. Click "System updates," and you'll see a message if there is an available update.

You may get the message that your phone is up to date, even if there are updates being sent to other users, because rolling updates will hit different phones at different times. At one point, there were three of us in my office with identical G1 phones. Our updates occurred more than a month apart from each other, even though we all had the same phone and carrier.

Don't worry about missing an update if you don't check. You'll receive an obvious alert that an update is available. Follow the instructions on the screen. It may take several minutes, but this does not mean your phone is broken. Your phone will usually restart after your firmware update is installed.

Alternatives to OTA

Yes, it's possible to manually install system updates in some cases. It may not be wise, and it may break your phone, void your warranty, or violate your carrier's terms of service. However, recent US copyright exceptions seem to indicate that it's not illegal to hack your phone to run on another network or run legally obtained software. If you're willing to take the risks and assume all responsibility for failure, the general process is not terribly complicated on most phones.

First you need to find an official update hosted from Google or another highly trusted source. On the Nexus One, the installation process for upgrading firmware goes like this:

1. Rename the zipped update file `update.zip`.

2. Transfer the update file to the top level of your SD card.

3. Restart your phone while holding the volume-down button.

4. You should see a text screen giving you several choices. Use the volume-down button to select Recovery, and press the power button.

5. When you see the triangle with the exclamation point, press the power button and then the volume-up button.

6. Select "apply sd card: update.zip." with your trackball, and then press the center of the trackball to begin.

7. You should see status updates and a progress bar as the update installs, and then your phone will either restart or you'll see the same screen you did when you pressed the power and volume-up buttons. If you see this screen, select "reboot."

8. Check your firmware status to make sure your phone has updated. If not try this process again.

You can find specific instructions and sometimes links to upgrade files on Phandroid's forums at http://androidforums.com.

Rooting Android

When you read about Android, you'll occasionally run into people who talk about "rooting" their phone. What this means is that they've hacked their phone to give them superuser or "root" access. This allows them to use modified versions of Android by "flashing" the phone with a new ROM and modifying the *bootloader*, or the process on Android and many other phones that loads the OS when you turn on the phone.

Users with rooted phones were able to use multitouch capabilities in Android before it was released, and 3G tethering before it became a feature in Android 2.2. If you have a phone that doesn't support Android 2.2, that still may be your only option.

If you're a developer, having a rooted phone allows you to test your apps on different devices by loading different images, including modified user interfaces from phone carriers.

However, there are some very big disadvantages to rooting your phone. The biggest and most obvious is that, if you do this process incorrectly, you may permanently break your phone (also known as "bricking" it). Not only would your phone be as useful as a brick, it would be broken while you're doing something that almost certainly voids your warranty and/or phone carrier's terms of service.

The danger doesn't just stop when you successfully gain root access. Your phone may overheat from performing tasks it wasn't meant to handle, you may lose data on your phone, or you may become the victim of malicious or just plain poorly written software.

Rooted phones also don't always get official OTA OS updates from phone carriers, so you'd be responsible for all phone maintenance. The chances of bricking your phone are probably slim, but it is a real risk, and certain modifications are riskier than others.

If you're still willing to take those risks, you can find instructions on T-Mobile's forums at http://forums.t-mobile.com/t5/Operating-System-Software/bd-p/AndroidDev, along with the very clear warning that using those user-supplied instructions voids your warranty. Most of their instructions would also apply to non-T-Mobile phones, but some phones, such as the DROID X, have additional security measures and a locked bootloader, so you will have to use a specialized DROID X rooting app.

CyanogenMod is probably one of the most popular mods users install on rooted Android phones. It allows tethering and multitouch on phones that don't support Android 2.2 along with other enhancements and features. You can find CyanogenMod at www.cyanogenmod.com.

Jailbreaking

Sometimes rooting Android is incorrectly referred to as "jailbreaking" in reference to a method of hacking iPhones. Jailbreaking iPhones is done to allow installation of third-party apps outside Apple's App Store. It's completely unnecessary on Android phones, because *there is no jail*. On an Android phone, go to the Home screen, press the Menu button, click Applications, and then check the box next to "Unknown sources." This allows you to install any Android app you'd like without going through the Android Market.

The term may be more appropriate when it refers to rooting eBook readers, such as the Barnes & Noble Nook eReader, that are locked off from accessing the Android Market or downloading third-party software. Not only are there more potential legal issues with someone who roots a device that comes with free wireless connectivity (which could be seen as theft of services), but Barnes & Noble or AT&T (the service provider) may simply solve the problem by finding a way to detect rooted Nooks and disconnect them from the network.

Resetting Your Phone

Sometimes you may have a phone that is crashing or behaving erratically. You may also want to give up your phone for a replacement or at the end of employment, and want to erase all your data. In such cases, you need to reset your phone.

There are two basic types or resets for your phone: hard and soft. A soft reset is like rebooting a computer, and relaunches the phone. A hard reset is like reformatting a computer's hard drive. It restores your phone to factory default settings, so only do this as a last resort.

Soft Reset

A soft reset happens every time you power your phone off and then turn it back on. If your phone is misbehaving, try holding down the power button and powering it off. If your phone is frozen to the point that the power button doesn't work, you can remove the battery. It's not a great habit to develop, so only do this if your phone is unresponsive for several minutes.

Hard Reset

A hard reset will wipe all your phone's data. This is ideal if you're selling the phone, but probably not the best choice if you want to keep the phone. In rare situations, you may find that your phone is unresponsive when you try to turn it on. It either hangs while booting up or crashes immediately after, and a soft reset will not fix the problem.

I'd recommend calling your carrier for support, but there are times when this is difficult and you need use of the phone right away. I found myself in this situation when I was traveling on a business trip. My phone would not advance beyond the bootup screen. I needed use of my phone more than I needed the specific configuration, so I ended up performing a hard reset.

If you do this correctly, it will not wipe your SIM card, but you *will* have to reenter all your Google account information and download your apps again. Different phones have different hard reset procedures. Phone manuals don't always include this, so you'll want to Google the specifics for your phone.

You generally need to hold down different keys while booting up—on the G1, these are the End and Home keys. On the Motorola DROID, these are the keyboard *X* and the power key; and after holding those down, you'll either have to hold more key combinations or navigate through a menu and select the format option. There's really no way to accidentally get to the hard reset option on your phone.

Once your phone is reset, it will be like you just opened it up from the box. It will ask for your Google account information and act as if it has never had an owner.

If you're resetting your phone to sell or return to an employer, also be sure to migrate all your files from your SD card to your computer by connecting it with a USB cable. Use your computer to then erase the files on the SD card when you're done. Alternatively, on many phones you can go through a hard reset and specify that you want to wipe the SD card instead. Be sure to also remove your SIM card if you plan on switching phones.

Reset Recovery

If you should be unfortunate enough to need a hard reset, don't panic. Yes, you will still have some work to set everything back up the way you had it. Your wallpaper and widget configurations will have been wiped. However, you will not have lost all your phone numbers.

You will still need to enter all your Google and Exchange account info by hand. However, your contact info has been syncing to Google Contacts all along, and your Exchange account has been syncing with an Exchange server, so once your phone knows which accounts to check, you'll be able to get that information back. In addition, the Android Market saves the information about which apps you've downloaded and purchased, so you can go back and download them again without having to pay twice.

You should still also have the information on your SIM and SD cards intact, even if you have to download a few apps again. That means your pictures and videos should still be intact, although the best bet would be to back them up regularly to avoid losing them.

Screen Captures from Android

You can take screen captures from your phone just like the screen captures you've seen in this book. Android offers its SDK as a free download from http://developer.android.com/sdk. You can find versions for Windows, Mac, and Linux. Part of the SDK is a Java app called Dalvik Debug Monitor Server (DDMS), which runs on your desktop. Developers can use it to debug their apps and also to make those handy screen captures that they upload to the Android Market. To take screen captures, perform the following steps:

1. Go to your Android phone. From the Home screen, press the Menu button, and then click Settings ➤ "Application settings" ➤ Development.

2. Check the box next to "USB debugging."

3. Go back to your computer desktop.

4. Launch DDMS from the Tools folder in the Android SDK.

5. Using your USB cable, connect your phone to your computer. You don't need to mount your SD card.

6. Use your phone to perform whatever action you want to capture.

7. Go to DDMS, and from the Device menu, select "Screen capture" (Figure 17–8).

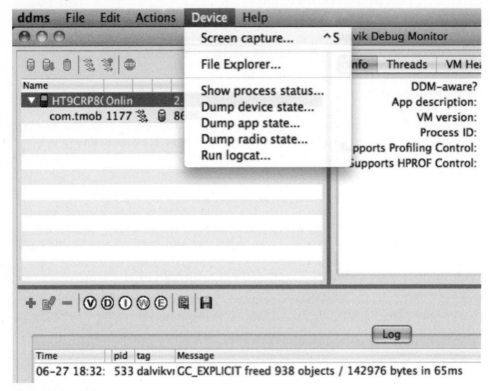

Figure 17–8. *DDMS*

You will capture whatever is on your phone screen at the time. You can save it as a PNG (Portable Network Graphics) file, and then click the refresh button for another screen capture.

Summary

Android's Home screen and widgets can be highly customized, and even Android itself is open to extreme hacking by those individuals who are willing to take the risks. Android also gives users the tools they need to manage their battery use and recover from most disasters, and, although you can completely reset your phone, it's difficult to do so by mistake.

As you explore the software and customization options, just remember to keep performance in mind. If you begin to see it lagging, try using the battery use and application information menus to pinpoint the problem and remove any problematic apps.

Resources for Managing Enterprise-Wide Android Deployment

When I began this book, the idea of enterprise-wide Android deployment seemed like something that would only happen in the distant future. Plenty of experts said that Android was not ready for prime-time and was not suitable for business use. Android was too young and lacked features required by business users. It may still be too young for the large enterprise to support.

If your enterprise uses Google Apps, an Android deployment is fairly simple, since Android has always been compatible with Google Apps accounts.

Google was listening to enterprise feedback as it developed Android 2.2 (Froyo). It features built-in support for Exchange autodiscovery, password policy enforcement, and remote data wiping. Google has also promised to slow down on rapid OS upgrades as Android becomes a stable platform for developers, so IT departments won't have to worry about managing upgrades every few months.

If you're planning on an enterprise rollout, you'll want to decide which Android phones you support. If you're supplying phones for deployment, it's an easier choice, since you can choose the model based on the features, carrier, and price.

If you're supporting employee choice, it becomes complicated. Phones running Android 1.6 are still being sold just as Android 2.2 is being rolled out, and several brand-new phones are being sold with modified versions of Android. Here are some resources to help you as you develop a policy for Android use and deployment:

- *NitroDesk (www.nitrodesk.com):*

  NitroDesk offers TouchDown, a corporate email app for Android. NitroDesk supports all versions of Android and works with Exchange 2003 and above, Zimbra, Kerio, GroupWise, and many other enterprise communication systems. NitroDesk also offers a volume license.

- *Quickoffice Connect (www.quickoffice.com/quickoffice_connect_suite_android):*

  This suite offers viewing and editing capabilities for Microsoft Office Word, Excel, and PowerPoint files. It also offers a volume licensing discount.

- *SMobile Systems (www.smobilesystems.com/business):*

  SMobile Systems is a mobile personal and enterprise security firm. It offers virus protection, GPS location, remote wipe, and "Monitor and Control" services for Android.

- *Android Security FAQ (http://developer.android.com/guide/appendix/faq/security.html):*

  This is a FAQ meant for Android developers.

- *Android Fragmentation: What It Means for You, Dear IT Manager (http://theemf.org/2010/05/24/android-fragmentation-what-it-means-for-you-dear-it-manager):*

  The EMF (Enterprise Mobility Foundation) explores enterprise use of mobile, and in this article it explores what the many variations of Android mean for your IT department.

- *Pyxis Mobile (http://pyxismobile.com/Platform/Index.aspx):*

  Pyxis offers a "MEAP" (Mobile Enterprise Application Platform), which allows developers to create an application once and deliver it on multiple platforms, including Android.

- *QR Code Generator (http://zxing.appspot.com/generator):*

  This is the ZXing Project's free QR code generator. If you need to distribute an app to multiple users, a QR code may be the most efficient way to do it at this point without major hacking. Android currently lacks good tools for mass configuration, but expect that to change in the near future.

- *Official Android site (www.android.com):*

  This is the official Android web site. It mainly serves as promotion for the Android platform, but it also includes videos and announcements about new Android features.

- *Android source code (http://source.android.com):*

  Here you can find the official Android source code, and the SDK is available here as well.

Resources for Developing Android Apps

Android apps are generally programmed in Java. Unlike the iPhone, anyone can download the Android SDK for free, and you can do your development from any computer you'd like. Google has been putting quite a bit of effort into recruiting Android programmers and has an extensive documentation available.

In order to offer items in the Android Market, you must pay a $25 registration fee. If you want to charge for your apps through the Android Market, you must have a merchant account with Google Checkout, which means you'll need to supply bank information and a tax ID number.

Google also sells carrier-independent developer's phones that you can use with your carrier's SIM card, although these phones don't offer all the latest features and software you'd get with a commercial phone. They may not even be running the latest version of Android.

Google App Inventor

Probably the most significant recent change in app development is Google App Inventor (http://appinventor.googlelabs.com). Google App Inventor allows non-programmers to create genuine Android apps by using a visual block-based programming interface based on MIT's OpenBlocks Java library. It's similar to the children's programming language Scratch.

App Inventor requires a Gmail account and an Android phone.

While App Inventor seems to do for Android development what WYSIWYG (what you see is what you get) HTML editors did for web design, it's not going to end traditional app development, and it's still a good idea to understand the foundations of Android development, just as most web designers understand HTML basics.

Web Resources for Android

Following are some valuable Android resources for developers:

- *Android Developers (*http://developer.android.com*):*

  The absolute first place to start is with the official Android Developers site. You can download the SDK and purchase a developer phone. You can also learn about developing for devices beyond phones, such as Google TV.

- *Eclipse (*www.eclipse.org/downloads*):*

  Android development is done in Java, and use of the Eclipse IDE (integrated development environment) is encouraged. You can download Eclipse for free.

- *Hello World (*http://developer.android.com/guide/tutorials/hello-world.html*):*

  Once you've downloaded Eclipse, you can return to Android Developers site for the Hello World tutorial. For programmers, "Hello World" refers to the first and most basic program you make in any language.

- *Stanford Engineering Everywhere (*http://see.stanford.edu/see/courses.aspx*):*

  Stanford University offers a variety of free courses on programming and engineering. The introductory programming course doesn't require any previous programming experience. If you're a programming newbie, this is a very solid start from the university where Google founders Sergey Brin and Larry Page met and got *their* start.

- *Stack Overflow (*http://stackoverflow.com/questions/tagged/android*):*

  Stack Overflow is a free programmer's question-and-answer user community. The link I provided goes directly to all questions tagged with Android. You're free to browse previous questions and answers or submit your own.

- *Anddev (*www.anddev.org*):*

  Anddev is a user community for developers. This community is organized as a forum (using phpBB, for those who are familiar with the platform). There are both "supervised" and open topics on a variety of Android development topics.

- *EuroDroid: "Google Android news from not-America"* (www.eurodroid.com):

  If you're a developer in the United States, this may not seem relevant, but Android phones are available worldwide, and many companies release the same phone to different markets at different times with only minor branding changes. It's possible to find solutions for American phones by browsing for information about their European counterparts.

Apress Books on Android

Following are some Apress titles that you can read to further your knowledge and understanding of Android:

- *Beginning Android*, by Mark Murphy: Learn how to develop applications for Android mobile devices using simple examples that are ready to run with your copy of the SDK. Author and Android columnist, writer, developer, and community advocate Mark Murphy shows you what you need to know to get started programming Android applications—everything from crafting GUIs to using GPS, accessing web services, and more!

- *Beginning Android 2*, by Mark Murphy: Learn how to develop applications for Android 2.x mobile devices.

- *Android Essentials*, by Chris Haseman: This book is a no-frills, no-nonsense, code-centric run through the guts of application development on Google's Mobile OS. This book uses the development of a sample application to work through topics, focusing on giving developers the essential tools and examples required to make viable commercial applications work. Since covering the entirety of the Android catalog in less than 150 pages is simply impossible, this book focuses on four main topics: the application life cycle and OS integration, the user interface, location-based services, and networking.

- *Pro Android*, by Satya Komatineni and Sayed Hashimi: This book takes a detailed look at application development on Google's Mobile OS. It uses the development of a sample application to work through everything you need to build a flexible mobile application. The focus is on making viable commercial applications work. The book includes detailed coverage of the Android API.

- *Pro Android 2*, by Satya Komatineni, Sayed Hashimi, and Dave MacLean: This book shows you how to build fun, real-world mobile applications using Google's Android SDK. It covers everything from the fundamentals of building applications for embedded devices to advanced concepts such as custom 3D components, OpenGL, and touchscreens including gestures.

- *Pro Android 3*, by Satya Komatineni, Dave MacLean, and Sayed Hashimi: This book takes a similar approach to *Pro Android 2*, but for Android 3. This yet-to-be-released version of Android is code named "Gingerbread" and will follow Android 2.2 "Froyo."

- *Practical Android Projects*, by Justin Bacon: Learn how to work with Android's incredible variety of tools and libraries to build your own cool and sophisticated Android apps.

- *Pro Android Web Apps: Developing HTML5, JavaScript, CSS, and Chrome OS Web Apps*, by Damon Oehlman: Web standards-based apps and web apps on mobile devices continues to grow for Android. This book teaches developers already familiar with web application development how to code and structure a web app for use on the Android mobile platform.

- *Beginning Android Games*, by Richard Taylor: This book offers everything you need to join the ranks of successful Android game developers. You'll start with game design fundamentals and programming basics, and then progress toward creating your own basic game engine and playable game.

- *Pro Android Media: Developing Graphics, Music, Video, and Rich Media Apps for Smartphones and Tablets*, by Shawn Van Every: This book provides concise and clear instruction on how to utilize the media APIs made available through Android to create dynamic apps.

Cross-Platform Development

Rather than developing for just Android, why not develop once and deliver to many different platforms? There are a growing number of tools and tutorials on doing just this:

- *PhoneGap (*www.phonegap.com*):*

    PhoneGap is an open source tool for developing phone apps in JavaScript, CSS, and HTML. The tool allows you to include features like vibration, sound, GPS, and the accelerometer into phone apps and write once for Android, Palm, Symbian, BlackBerry, and iPhone.

- *MoSync (*www.mosync.com*):*

  MoSync is an open source project similar to PhoneGap, but it is not free. Its license includes free home use, but the company sells developer licenses.

- *RhoMobile (*http://rhomobile.com*):*

  RhoMobile offers data hosting and cross-platform development tools using HTML and Ruby.

- *Adobe Device Central (*www.adobe.com/products/creativesuite/devicecentral*):*

  Adobe Flash runs on Android, but not the iPhone. However, Adobe has been working on cross-platform solutions using AIR, and ways to create once and deliver on multiple platforms using the Device Central component of its CS5 software (e.g., Photoshop and Premiere).

Apress Titles for Cross-Platform Development

Following are some additional titles you can read to learn more about cross-platform development:

- *Pro Smartphone Cross-Platform Development: iPhone, BlackBerry, Windows Mobile, and Android Development and Distribution*, by Vidal Graupera, Sarah Allen, and Lee Lundrigan: Learn the theory behind cross-platform development, and put the theory into practice with code using the invaluable information presented in this book. With in-depth coverage of development and distribution techniques for iPhone, BlackBerry, Windows Mobile, and Android, you'll learn the native approach to working with each of these platforms.

- *Beginning Smartphone Web Development: Building JavaScript, CSS, HTML, and Ajax-Based Applications for iPhone, Android, Palm Pre, BlackBerry, Windows Mobile, and Nokia S60*, by Gail Frederick and Rajesh Lal: By the end of this book, you'll have the training, tools, and techniques for creating robust mobile web experiences on a wide array of platforms for your favorite smartphone or other mobile device.

Other Resources for Android

Finally, here are some additional resources for learning more about Android:

- *andbook!*, by Nicolas Gramlich (http://andbook.anddev.org): This is a free eBook based on experiences from the Anddev.org user community.

- *Safari Books Online (*http://my.safaribooksonline.com*):*

  This is a subscription service for training books and tutorial videos. Think Netflix for tech books. This book and other Apress titles are available through the service for a monthly fee, although a phone app for book browsing is not yet available.

- *Hello, Android: Introducing Google's Mobile Development Platform*, by Ed Burnette (Pragmatic Bookshelf, 2008): This book focuses on practical exercises to teach beginning programmers how to create Android apps.

- *Teach Yourself Java 6 in 21 Days*, by Rogers Cadenhead and Laura Lemay (Sams, 2007): This book is not about Android. It's designed to teach beginners the basics of Java, which will then make it easier to understand Android when you look at other books and tutorials.

Index

You Need the Companion eBook

Your purchase of this book entitles you to buy the companion PDF-version eBook for only $10. Take the weightless companion with you anywhere.

We believe this Apress title will prove so indispensable that you'll want to carry it with you everywhere, which is why we are offering the companion eBook (in PDF format) for $10 to customers who purchase this book now. Convenient and fully searchable, the PDF version of any content-rich, page-heavy Apress book makes a valuable addition to your programming library. You can easily find and copy code—or perform examples by quickly toggling between instructions and the application. Even simultaneously tackling a donut, diet soda, and complex code becomes simplified with hands-free eBooks!

Once you purchase your book, getting the $10 companion eBook is simple:

❶ Visit **www.apress.com/promo/tendollars/**.

❷ Complete a basic registration form to receive a randomly generated question about this title.

❸ Answer the question correctly in 60 seconds, and you will receive a promotional code to redeem for the $10.00 eBook.

THE EXPERT'S VOICE™

233 Spring Street, New York, NY 10013